Enter Into God's Rest ...
But Not in English Class

Enter Into God's Rest ...
But Not in English Class

MARTHA BOLTON

SERVANT PUBLICATIONS
ANN ARBOR, MICHIGAN

Vine Books is an imprint of Servant Publications especially designed to
serve evangelical Christians.

Published by Servant Publications
P.O. Box 8617
Ann Arbor, Michigan 48107

Cover design by Paz Design Group-Salem, Oregon

01 02 03 04 10 9 8 7 6 5 4 3 2 1

Printed in the United States of America
ISBN 1-56955-233-9

Library of Congress Cataloging-in-Publication Data

Bolton, Martha, 1951 -
    Enter into God's rest—but not in English class / Martha Bolton.
        p. cm.
    ISBN 1-56955-233-9
        1. Christian teenagers—Prayer-books and devotions—English.
2. Bible. N.T. Hebrews—Devotional literature. [1. Prayer books and
devotions.] I. Title.

    BV4850 .B62 2001
    242'.63—dc21

                                                    2001020968

Dedicated to
Martha Przybyla
A sister by friendship

Contents

One
▲▼▲

Stand-Up Christian

I work with a lot of stand-up comics. I admire many of them for their talent. I admire all of them for their courage. It's not easy to stand up and tell joke after joke with the audience's opinion of you hanging on each punch line. It takes guts.

I admire people who stand up in another way, too. Those who have the courage to stand up for others. Jesus stood up for others. He stood up for those who were being picked on, gossiped about, or unfairly judged. That woman who was caught in adultery? Jesus stood up for her. He didn't stand up for her sin, but he stood up for her. It wasn't politically correct to do so, but Jesus knew she was better than her failures. She was a person worthy of his love, and ultimately his life. He stood up for her regardless of how much it might cost him, politically or physically.

Jesus stood up for Zaccheus, too. As a tax collector, Zaccheus didn't have a lot of friends. He was ridiculed and despised. Yet out of all those more socially acceptable people, it was Zaccheus that Jesus approached. Not the religious leaders. Not the politicians. Not even the rich or famous. It was Zaccheus, the tax collector. Jesus invited himself over to Zaccheus' house for dinner, and didn't even ask around to see what kind of a cook Zaccheus was.

So, be like Jesus. Be the kind of friend who will defend the weak and speak up for those who can't, for whatever reason, speak up for themselves. Don't stand by silently when someone is being picked on or gossiped about. Be a stand-up friend. It may take a little extra courage, but stand-up friendship is the only friendship that really counts.

Thoughts to Ponder

When someone you know is being gossiped about or unfairly judged, do you tend to stand up for that person or remain silent?

How does it make you feel when you hear about someone who stood up for you behind your back?

Bumper Sticker for the Day

> **Sometimes the defense shouldn't rest.**

Scripture to Stand On

For ye had compassion of me in my bonds.

HEBREWS 10:34, KJV

Hello Again, Lord ...

Lord, forgive me for when I haven't stood up for others like I should have, and for when I haven't stood up for you.

Two
▲▼▲

Cardboard Armor

Have you ever watched how luggage is handled at some airports? After the clerk throws it onto the conveyor belt, it is tossed onto a luggage cart and driven recklessly to the airplane, where it's heaved onto another conveyor belt that bounces it up to the luggage compartment under the plane.... Who knows what happens to it after that?

Then, if you have a plane change, your suitcase gets taken off that plane, tossed onto one more luggage cart, driven to your connecting flight, and thrown into that luggage compartment.

That's not even counting all of the turbulence it might have to endure while in the air.

When you finally arrive at your destination, your suitcase gets taken off the plane, tossed onto yet another luggage cart, driven to the baggage claim section, then thrown onto a conveyor belt, where a succession of passengers lift it, examine it to see if it's theirs, then toss it back.

After all of this, it finally reaches you—sometimes in one piece, sometimes in several pieces. It all depends on the quality of the suitcase. Good luggage can usually take it. It will absorb the shock and protect whatever valuables are inside. Flimsy cardboard suitcases simply fall apart.

Did you know trust in God is like good luggage? It helps us to absorb the shock, the mishandling, and the turbulence of life. We can trust God to cover us with his protective arms and keep safe the valuables that are inside.

Don't trust in the flimsy, undependable, cardboard things of life to protect you. You're on a long, sometimes turbulent journey. Pack your life in the Best.

Thoughts to Ponder

Have you been feeling as if you were "falling apart" lately?

Why do you think it's important to safeguard your life by putting your trust in God?

Bumper Sticker for the Day

You're valuable to God.
He'll take care of what's valuable to you.

Scripture to Stand On

And again, "I will put my trust in him."

HEBREWS 2:13

Hello Again, Lord ...

Lord, sometimes life can get rough. Thank you for absorbing most of the shock.

Three
▲▼▲

Great Expectations

A friend of mine had a car accident. She didn't hit another car. She didn't hit a pedestrian. She didn't even hit a tree. She was driving along a freeway one night, minding her own business, and hit a recliner.

That's right. A recliner. For some unknown reason, there was a recliner in the middle of her lane. She tried her best to swerve and miss it, but there hadn't been enough warning. Evidently, there weren't any "Recliner Crossing" or "Watch For Falling Easy Chairs" signs posted by the side of the highway.

Now, in all the years that I've been driving, I've never had to swerve to avoid a recliner. I have, however, swerved to avoid other things, like cattle, a herd of moose, a spilled truckload of canned beets, and squirrels who couldn't quite make up their minds whether to cross the street. Just like that recliner, none of these other road hazards were expected either.

Driver's training or driver's education classes can't possibly cover everything you might encounter on the road. They simply tell you to be prepared for anything and everything.

Much of life can come as a total surprise. We didn't expect our parents to get a divorce. We didn't know our pet was going to die. We had no way of guessing when our teacher was going to give us that pop quiz. We had no idea that instant tanning cream would turn us the color of Tang. The unexpected *is* going to happen. All we can do is try our best to be prepared for it.

Good things often come as a surprise, too. We didn't know we were going to win that award, or find that prize token for a free bag of French fries, or a thousand other unexpected good things.

So don't just set your life on cruise control. Stay alert. Prepare for the unexpected. It will come. It always does, both the good and the bad. If you're looking ahead, and believe in God's ultimate goodness, you'll be able to handle it all.

Thoughts to Ponder

Think of an unexpected crisis you had to face recently. In what ways could you have better prepared yourself for it?

Think of some unexpected good news that recently came your way. Why do you think it's easier for people to remember unexpected problems than unexpected blessings?

Bumper Sticker for the Day

God is God of the unexpected, too.

Scripture to Stand On

We have this hope as an anchor for the soul, firm and secure.

HEBREWS 6:19

Hello Again, Lord ...

Lord, life is unpredictable. I am thankful that you are the same yesterday, today, and forever.

Four
▲▼▲

Memory Loss

Have you ever forgotten something? It could be your locker combination, where you left your glasses, what day it is, or what time you were supposed to take those brownies out of the oven (the fire department usually reminds me of that last one).

I once forgot all about a national radio interview that I was supposed to do. I had been in California for some surgery, then flew home to Nashville, and drove the next day to east Tennessee, where I was teaching comedy. That put me in three different time zones in a twenty-four-hour period. I'm lucky I remembered my name.

For the entire three-and-a-half-hour drive to east Tennessee, I didn't think once about the radio interview I was supposed to be doing at three o'clock that day. But by the time I got to work, I had an answering tape full of embarrassing reminders.

"We're trying to reach Martha Bolton. She has a radio interview scheduled in five minutes."

"Martha, where are you? You're supposed to be on the air."

"Please call us, Martha. We've been announcing you for the show. It's now 3:15. Call us."

"It's now 3:27. Call us."

"It's now 3:35. Call us."

The messages came at regular intervals until 4:00. I felt sick to my stomach. I couldn't believe I had forgotten an interview! Luckily, Kolleen O'Meara, the publicist, was able to explain what had happened, and the radio station was understanding and gave me a second chance.

Forgetting appointments, our homework, or where we live isn't good. It's frustrating to know that our brains don't always work like date books or PalmPilots. Yet, forgetting about our failures, other than what we can learn from them, can be both healthy and healing.

When God promises to forget our wrongs, he means it. It's not like having to be reminded of a radio interview, or forgetting where I put my glasses and eventually remembering I left them in my shirt pocket. He totally forgets our wrongs. Just like when you shake a picture away on an Etch A Sketch. It's gone, and all you're left with is a clean slate.

Thoughts to Ponder

When God promises to not only forgive your sins, but not even remember them, how does that make you feel?

Are you wasting your life remembering your forgiven sins, or are you seeing yourself as God does—a clean slate?

Bumper Sticker for the Day

When God deletes your sins, they're unretrievable.

Scripture to Stand On

And their sins and iniquities will I remember no more.

HEBREWS 10:17

Hello Again, Lord ...

Thanks, Lord, for remembering your promises and forgetting our failures.

Five

▲▼▲

A Change in Direction

Sometimes we find ourselves doing the exact opposite of what we should do, don't we? Why do we do it? Who knows? The important thing is recognizing how much our negative behavior complicates our lives, and taking steps to stop it.

The following prayer might help you do just that!

Lord, help me not to...

step back when I need to step out;
let go when I need to hold on;
put down when I need to lift up;
give in when I need to walk out;
turn back when I need to go on;
speed up when I need to slow down;
withhold when I need to give back;
stay home when I need to show up;
pull back when I need to reach out;
let down when I need to come through;
speak out when I need to hush up;
sit down when I need to stand up;
clam up when I need to speak out;
run off when I need to stay put;
be down when I need to look up;
give up when I need to kneel down.

Thoughts to Ponder

Can you think of a situation when you did the opposite of what you were supposed to do?

If the situation were to come up again, what do you think you would do differently this time?

Bumper Sticker for the Day

> Doing the wrong thing is tough.
> All that rationalization can take hours.

Scripture to Stand On

May the God of peace, who through the blood of the eternal covenant brought back from the dead our Lord Jesus, that great Shepherd of the sheep, equip you with everything good for doing his will, and may he work in us what is pleasing to him, through Jesus Christ, to whom be glory for ever and ever. Amen.

HEBREWS 13:20-21

Hello Again, Lord ...

Lord, I have a choice in the things that I do. Help me to choose the right ones.

Six

▲▼▲

Enough is Enough

Have you ever wondered when it's OK to stop caring about people? Is it when they change churches and no longer go to the one we attend? As long as they were in our youth group or attending our Sunday morning worship services, they were on our hearts and minds. Yet if they start attending church elsewhere, we hardly ever think about them, much less pray for them. Out of sight, out of mind. And anyway, let their new church handle their prayer needs. We've got enough problems of our own, right?

Maybe it's OK to stop caring when people slip up in their Christian walk. Again. And again. And again. The Lord knows, we've given them plenty of chances, but they keep messing up. They make wrong decision after wrong decision, and, well, to be perfectly honest, their lives are looking hopeless. They're never going to change. Once we've made that determination, it's time to stop caring, isn't it?

Or perhaps it's when we've been given so many negative critiques about them from all our one-sided, very-nearly-reliable sources that we're afraid to even talk to that person anymore, much less care for him or her.

Or maybe it's out of our loyalty to someone else, or fear of that person, that we stop caring. After all, if friend #1 found out we were nice to friend #2, he or she might quit talking to us. We certainly couldn't make a sacrifice like that.

So, when can we stop caring about someone? If we really

want the answer to this, we'll have to look at Christ's example. He didn't stop caring until it cost him everything.

Thoughts to Ponder

Have you ever stopped caring about someone because of his or her behavior, or because of outside pressures?

Why do you think loving God's way means giving up all of our excuses for not caring about someone?

Bumper Sticker for the Day

> God's love isn't subject to outside forces.
> The love we show others shouldn't be, either.

Scripture to Stand On

And do not forget to do good and to share with others, for with such sacrifices God is pleased.

HEBREWS 13:16

Hello Again, Lord ...

Lord, help me to forgive others as many times as I'd want you to forgive me.

Seven

▲▼▲

High-Flying Faith

I took my four-year-old granddaughter, Kiana, to an Easter pageant recently. It was a moving reenactment of Jesus' final week on earth. The beginning of the play may have been a bit over her head, but she sat wide-eyed and breathless through the crucifixion, resurrection, and transfiguration scenes.

After the play, she had a few questions. She wanted to know why all those people were yelling at Jesus, why he had to die, and then, "Can Jesus fly?"

She was referring, of course, to the transfiguration scene. In that scene, the actor playing the role of Jesus had been secured in a harness and was, at the proper moment, lifted to heaven, or as far as the roof would allow, anyway.

Kiana was impressed.

"Can Jesus fly?" she pressed. "Can he?"

"Well, he did fly to heaven after he came back to life," I told her. "And the Bible says that someday he'll come back to earth riding on the clouds."

Her eyes grew even bigger.

"I want to fly like Jesus," she said.

"You do?" I said.

She nodded excitedly, then paused for a moment and quickly added, "But I don't want that cross part."

To a four-year-old child, the flying to heaven aspect of the gospel looked like fun. But the cross? Well, that was a different story.

Even the disciples debated over who would sit at Jesus' right hand in heaven; yet, who was at his right hand as he stood before Pilate?

Most of us are the same way. We want the spiritual perks that come with being a believer, but we'd rather pass on the sacrifices. We want to "fly like Jesus," but we don't want "that cross part."

Thoughts to Ponder

Are you willing to make sacrifices for your faith?

Name a sacrifice you've made this week for your faith.

Bumper Sticker for the Day

> Jesus—his tomb is empty, but not his promises.

Scripture to Stand On

He regarded disgrace for the sake of Christ as of greater value than the treasures of Egypt, because he was looking ahead to his reward.

HEBREWS 11:26

Hello Again, Lord ...

Lord, don't ever let me forget what my entrance into heaven cost you.

Eight

▲▼▲

The High Road

When I was a teenager, my cousin Lynn, who was my age, would often spend the night at my house. Just before we'd drift off to sleep, we'd take turns singing. Well, actually, Lynn would sing more than I did. Our town had strict laws about disturbing the peace. Contrary to my voice, Lynn's was soothing. I loved to fall asleep listening to her sing a song called "The Banks of Loch Lohman." The lyrics went something like this:

> You take the high road and I'll take the low road
> And I'll get to Scotland a'fore ye
> For me and my true love will never meet again
> on those bonny, bonny banks of Loch Lohman.

OK, so it wasn't a top-ten hit, but it's a fond memory for me, especially since Lynn died when we were both fourteen years old. To this day I still catch myself humming those lyrics and remembering the laughs and good times we shared.

In most circumstances, there are two roads we can take—the high road and the low road. The low road is often the most tempting. If someone hurts us, we want to hurt that person back. If someone gossips about us, we want to gossip about him or her. If someone acts judgmental about our failures, we want to rent a billboard and list that person's failings. Maybe even two billboards.

But that's the low road. Sure, it's temporarily satisfying, but it won't take us very far in life. The high road is the better choice. By taking the high road, we're not saying that other people's actions haven't hurt us, or that what they did wasn't wrong. We're simply saying that life's too interesting a journey to waste it the way they're wasting it, acting the way they're acting.

The high road or the low road—the choice is ours. But the scenery and the company are always better on the high road. Do everything you can to stay on it.

Thoughts to Ponder

Why do you think some people prefer to live life on the low road?

What do you think you'll gain by taking the high road when it comes to confrontations or conflict?

Bumper Sticker for the Day

> Hate crowds? Take the high road.
> Not that many people travel it anymore.

Scripture to Stand On

Therefore, since we are surrounded by such a great cloud of witnesses, let us throw off everything that hinders and the sin that so easily entangles, and let us run with perseverance the race marked out for us.

HEBREWS 12:1

Hello Again, Lord ...

Lord, when I have a choice, help me to always take the high road.

Nine

▲▼▲

Here We Go Again

Do you have a recurring problem in your life? Something you keep trying to overcome, but can't seem to? Or maybe it's a personality type. Is there one particular personality type that seems to keep showing up to make your life more difficult than it needs to be?

When a physical therapist works with a person, they try to get that person to build up the muscle that's been injured or weakened in some way. The other muscles are working fine. It's the weak one that needs strengthening.

Did you ever wonder if maybe that's why the same problems keep showing up in your life? Maybe the muscles you need to deal with that problem or personality type are too weak. If so, you may find that you keep going back to the same problem, or you end one bad relationship only to end up in another. We all need to keep our total selves fit, but sometimes we need a little special attention to certain areas.

If you have a difficult time around rude, confrontational people, yet they seem to keep popping up in your life, perhaps you need to learn how to confront a few people yourself. Only you'll want to do it in the right way. If you keep finding yourself drawn to unhealthy relationships, maybe it's your self-esteem muscle that needs a little attention.

If you're having a hard time saying no, but find yourself often in the company of those who take advantage of you, God might be saying you need a little more practice at setting boundaries.

After a debilitating accident, physical therapy can help us learn to walk again. Building up our good decision, boundary setting, and self-esteem muscles gets back our spiritual and emotional standing, too.

Thoughts to Ponder

Do you have a recurring problem or personality type with which you have difficulty dealing?

What do you think you can learn from each encounter with this person or problem?

Bumper Sticker for the Day

> When we're out of spiritual shape,
> all our problems look overwhelming.

Scripture to Stand On

Let us hold unswervingly to the hope we profess, for he who promised is faithful.

HEBREWS 10:23

Hello Again, Lord ...

Lord, thank you for being the best personal trainer we can have for life.

Ten

▲▼▲

No Barbie

While shopping at a store once, I turned a corner and was greeted with a gruff, "What are you looking at?" I continued to make my way up the aisle amidst even more rude comments.

"What's your problem?"

"Take a hike!"

"Get outta my face!"

And so on. It took a while, but I finally found the source of the crabbiness. It was a talking doll sitting on the top shelf. I forget the name of the doll, but it sure had an attitude problem. It had about ten or twelve different rude sayings that it would spew at whoever happened to walk too close to it.

By the time I made my way down that aisle, that doll had taken my good mood and wreaked havoc on it. I wanted to run it over with my shopping cart ... several times. How dare it talk to a perfect stranger like that? What was its problem, anyway? Sure, it was just a doll, but manners are manners.

I didn't run it over or hire a hit doll to do it in. I didn't do anything but ignore it. After all, the doll was only saying what was inside of it.

The Bible tells us that what's inside of us is going to come out of our mouths, too. If we're filled with anger, hurt, lack of forgiveness, bitterness, pride, or a judgmental attitude, that's what's going to come out of our mouths. Just like that doll was programmed to make rude comments, our attitude preprograms the words that leave our lips, too.

However, if we're filled with love, joy, understanding, long-suffering, humility, and an attitude of forgiving others as we want to be forgiven ourselves, then the words coming from our mouths will reflect that same attitude. This will be true of both what we say publicly and what we say privately.

And just for the record, that doll's a lot nicer now. Unless, of course, someone found the batteries and put them back in.

Thoughts to Ponder

Are you proud of what's inside of you?

If not, what steps can you take toward changing that which is inside of you?

Bumper Sticker for the Day

Character is like catsup—
give it a good squeeze and it'll come out.

Scripture to Stand On

Let us draw near to God with a sincere heart in full assurance of faith, having our hearts sprinkled to cleanse us from a guilty conscience and having our bodies washed with pure water.

HEBREWS 10:22

Hello Again, Lord ...

Lord, help me to surrender my all to you—who I am on the outside and who I am on the inside, too.

Eleven

▲▼▲

Stitches

Over the years I've had to endure my share of stitches, or, as I like to refer to them, "body embroidery."

When I was seven years old, I raced one of my sisters to our car and jumped in, hitting my head on the frame and busting it open about an inch. (My head, not the frame.) A line of stitches was needed to close it back up and keep what brains I have, inside.

I've received stitches for various cuts on my hands, feet, and numerous other body parts, as well. In fact, I don't really know how many stitches have been sewed into my body. Yet I do know this—not one stitch is still there today. Why? Because stitches are only a temporary help. They're meant to hold your skin together only until it can properly heal and stay together on its own. Once it has, they'll either dissolve on their own or have to be removed by a doctor. As good and as medically sound as stitches are, there comes a time when they need to come out. If they're allowed to stay in, the stitches themselves can become irritated and end up causing more problems than they solve.

When we get hurt by life, stitches help us heal, too. One such stitch is self-pity. A brief period of self-pity is perfectly normal. Some of the things that happen to us in life aren't fair, and it's no doubt healthy to acknowledge the unfairness. Yet if we leave that stitch in too long, the stitch itself can end up hurting us.

Another stitch that can help us during hard times is leaning on others. Pastors, counselors, and support groups can all help us through difficult times. They can be available to us 24-7. For a while. Yet we shouldn't become totally dependent on their help, either. The key word here is "totally." These people want to be there for us whenever we need them, but if we wear them out over just one problem, what are we going to do when the next problem comes up?

Just as you know when your physical wounds are healing, you should be able to tell when your emotional ones are healing, too. Recognize that, and go ahead and pull out the stitches. Not too soon, of course. But certainly not too late.

Thoughts to Ponder
Are you nursing a wound that you feel has already healed? Why do you think you're afraid to take out the "stitches"?

What could be the possible benefits if you were to remove those "stitches"?

Bumper Sticker for the Day

> A safety net is a nice place to land,
> but you shouldn't want to live there.

Scripture to Stand On
Therefore strengthen your feeble arms and weak knees.

HEBREWS 12:12

Hello Again, Lord ...
Lord, I know you understand my every hurt, but help me to recognize when you've healed them.

Twelve

▲▼▲

Perfect Builder

My father was a carpenter. Whenever we'd drive around town, Dad would point out the various homes, office buildings, or malls on which he'd worked. "I did the cabinetry in that one," he'd say. Or, "I put the stairs in that one." Or, "You should see the doors I hung in that one."

I wonder if Joseph ever took Jesus around Nazareth and showed him the different homes, stores, or boats that he had worked on. Whether he did or not, Jesus knew what it was like to grow up in a carpenter's home, to watch a pile of wood turn into something of beauty and usefulness. He knew what it was like to be tucked into bed by a carpenter's hands, calloused and dry from handling rough lumber or branches, or to be held in a carpenter's strong arms.

I'm sure Joseph, like my father, made things for Jesus to take to school for show and tell, and every year on his birthday Jesus no doubt received special handmade gifts, just like I did.

I've always felt a connection to Jesus on that level. We had something in common during our formative years. Of course, Jesus no doubt built some incredible pieces himself, amazing everyone who saw them. The things I made didn't do that. Like the "Leaning Tower of Bookshelves" I made one summer, or the collapsible chair I built that wasn't meant to collapse.

Still, to make something out of nothing, to build a cabinet out of unfinished wood, or to cut and sew a dress or shirt out of a bolt of material, or to write a story on blank pieces of paper, gives the creator of such things a real sense of accomplishment. Imagine, though, creating every single thing that we see on Earth—all the plant life, the animals, the fish, and man—and creating the sun, moon, every single star, planet, and galaxy, and making them all operate in perfect harmony. Now that's impressive. God did that, Jesus' real father. And I'm sure Jesus talked about him on share day, too.

Thoughts to Ponder

What things do you think you might have in common with Jesus during his teen years?

List some of the same challenges you think Jesus might have faced as a teenager, as teens face today.

Bumper Sticker for the Day

God's creations never get recalled.

Scripture to Stand On

For every house is built by someone, but God is the builder of everything.

HEBREWS 3:4

Hello Again, Lord ...

Jesus, sometimes I forget that you were once a teenager, too. Not only do you care about my problems, but you understand them, too...

Thirteen

▲▼▲

True Intelligence

He was a slow learner.

When someone was needed to introduce the mayor, who spoke at the Easter morning service at our church, no one thought of asking him to do it. After all, he would no doubt stumble over his words.

They let him join the church choir, but the director hid him on the top row, left corner, far away from the microphones. He'd be safe there. He was a slow learner and had trouble reading the sheet music. He couldn't sing in tune so he was never given a solo, of course, and on more than one occasion, they "accidentally" forgot to tell him about a choir party they were having. He never suspected anything. After all, he was a slow learner.

He joined the church basketball team and cheered faithfully for his teammates, jumping up to give them a high five after every successful play. It was easy to do that from the bench. At least he got to be part of the team, wear the uniform, and pose for pictures. He was a slow learner who wouldn't really know the difference between actually playing and "sitting this one out."

When it came time for the annual day of prayer and everyone else signed up for the premium hours, passing over the 2-3 A.M., 3-4 A.M., and 4-5 A.M. slots, he printed his name in large block letters next to all three. He didn't know the difference. He was a slow learner.

When a homeless man wandered into our church one Sunday night, dirty and smelly, he was the first to shake his hand and welcome him. And he was the only one who didn't wash his hands afterward. He didn't know there was a difference between a friendly handshake and a guarded one because, well, you know, he was a slow learner.

He died alone in his one-room apartment. Only a handful took the time to attend his funeral. There were more important things to do. But when he walked through those pearly gates, the cheers he heard were louder than at any earthly ball game. The angelic choir director placed him front row center where all of heaven could see and hear him. And there wasn't a single heavenly celebration to which he wasn't invited. Then, Jesus himself took him by the hand and personally escorted him to his mansion—the biggest and best one on the block—walking right past all those "religious folk" who had slighted him on earth. Confused, the man turned to Jesus and asked why he was being treated so much better than those who had been blessed with far greater earthly intelligence and influence. Jesus smiled and said, "They were slow learners."

Thoughts to Ponder

Have you ever been guilty of looking down on someone who didn't rise to your "social standards"?

Why do you think Jesus wants us to judge people by their hearts alone?

Bumper Sticker for the Day

> Never look down on anybody.
> God could easily reverse the view.

Scripture to Stand On

And let us consider how we may spur one another on toward love and good deeds.

HEBREWS 10:24

Hello Again, Lord ...

Lord, forgive me for those times when I've failed to see people through your eyes and heart.

Fourteen

▲▼▲

One In Every Crowd

No doubt you've heard the expression, "There's one in every crowd." One what? Well, in almost any grouping of people, you can usually find at least one doubter, betrayer, whiner, or some other difficult personality type. It's not scientific, but it does seem to happen that way. Some of us, like Jesus, have even had to deal with more than one. Jesus had Judas. He also had the Pharisees. Joshua and Caleb had the ten unfaithful spies. Who do you have? Is there someone in your circle of friends or acquaintances who seems to be less encouraging than others? Is there one who's more critical, negative, or jealous? Is there someone who, like Joshua at the walls of Jericho, is just waiting for you to fall?

None of us are going to be loved and esteemed by every single person with whom we happen to come into contact. Jesus wasn't, and he was perfect. Since we aren't perfect, it's reasonable to assume that there'll be at least one difficult person in our lives. The key is not to let them get us down.

Jesus didn't let Judas' behavior sidetrack him. He could have been so hurt over what Judas had done that it interfered with his mission. He could have wondered "How could Judas do this to me? He was a friend, my treasurer. Is this how he repays my trust?"

But he didn't.

Jesus didn't let the Pharisees sidetrack him either. He knew his mission and followed it in spite of how much Judas had let him down. By keeping his mind on what he needed to do, Jesus was able to complete the assignment God had ordained for him.

God has a plan for your life, too. Yes, you may have a few doubters, discouragers, even betrayers in your life, but don't let them take your mind off your mission.

Thoughts to Ponder

When you think of your circle of friends and acquaintances, is there someone who doesn't seem to have your best interest at heart?

Do you spend more of your day fretting over that person, or following your calling?

Bumper Sticker for the Day

Reward your friends—not your enemies—
with your time and attention.

Scripture to Stand On

Since that time he waits for his enemies to be made his footstool.

HEBREWS 10:13

Hello Again, Lord ...

Lord, help me to stay on track with your purpose for my life.

Fifteen

▲▼▲

To Tell the Truth

Do you know God can't lie? It's not just that he simply doesn't want to. He can't. The book of Hebrews tells us that it is impossible for God to lie. It's his nature to tell the truth. So then...

—if God can't lie, when he says he loves us, he means it.

—if God can't lie, when he says he has a plan for our lives, he means it.

—if God can't lie, when he says we're all equal in his sight, he means it.

—if God can't lie, when he says he wants to bless us, he means it.

—if God can't lie, when he says he'll give us the desires of our heart, he means it.

—if God can't lie, when he says we can trust him, he means it.

—if God can't lie, when he says he'll never leave us, he means it.

—if God can't lie, when he says he'll give us peace, he means it.

—if God can't lie, when he says there's a price to be paid for sin, he means it.

—if God can't lie, when he says the cross bought our forgiveness, he means it.

—if God can't lie, when he says the gospel is all about grace, he means it.

—if God can't lie, when he says there's a heaven, he means it.

—if God can't lie, when he says there's a hell, he means it.

—if God can't lie, when he says one day every knee will bow before him, he means it.

—if God can't lie, when he says the best is yet to come for those who believe in him, he means it!

Thoughts to Ponder

What are some other truths that God has given to us in the Bible?

How does it make you feel to know that when God says something, it's an unchangeable fact?

Bumper Sticker for the Day

> God gave his word on his Word.

Scripture to Stand On

God did this so that, by two unchangeable things in which it is impossible for God to lie, we who have fled to take hold of the hope offered to us may be greatly encouraged.

HEBREWS 6:18

Hello Again, Lord ...

Lord, thank you for being a God of your word.

Sixteen

▲▼▲

Choice of the Month

I used to belong to a book-of-the-month club. If you're feeling bad because you don't get enough mail, join a book club. Book clubs are terrific at corresponding. They'll faithfully write to you several times a month, whether you want them to or not. Even if you move, they'll track you down. I think they have former FBI agents working in their customer service department.

One of the mailings they'll send is a packet outlining that month's featured reading selections. The packet will also include a card for you to mark, indicating whether you want "This month's featured selection," "Another selection," or "No book." If you don't return the card, the featured book will automatically come to you, so it's a good idea to return the card. If they don't hear from you, they assume you want the book.

It's also a good idea to let others know what we don't want when it comes to life choices. "I don't want to do drugs." "I don't want to cheat on my exams." "I don't want to do things that are harmful to my body or my reputation."

I'm not saying we have to rent billboard space and announce our standards to the world. Yet we can easily get the message out by the things we say and by how we act.

Making our literary desires known helps to keep unwanted books from showing up in our mail. Making our life choices known can keep a lot of temptation away, too.

Thoughts to Ponder

Do you think your friends know your standards?

In what subtle or obvious ways do you think you could start reinforcing your standards to those around you?

Bumper Sticker for the Day

> Just say no ... because only thinking it
> isn't always enough.

Scripture to Stand On

See to it, brothers, that none of you has a sinful, unbelieving heart that turns away from the living God.

HEBREWS 3:12

Hello Again, Lord ...

Lord, help me to remember that sometimes it's easier to say no long before I'm asked.

Seventeen

▲▼▲

Holy Laughter

I used to be a church secretary. I wasn't your usual church secretary, as the pastor I worked for would freely attest to. I was constantly playing pranks on him. And he on me. I recall one April Fool's Day in particular when I arranged for numerous salespeople and one pizza delivery boy to show up at his house unannounced. This went on for the entire day, a steady stream of people, from vacuum cleaner salesmen to insurance salesmen to you name it.

Once he finally figured out who the culprit was behind all the interruptions on his day off, it was payback time. When my husband and I returned home from dinner that evening, we discovered that he (at least I'm fairly certain it was our pastor) had neatly arranged a week's worth of his trash on my front porch. I, of course, got back at him by pulling yet another prank, followed by yet another one from him. I forget what time it was when we finally decided to call a truce, but I do remember all the laughs we shared that day and on many days since, just recalling it.

My husband and I have worked closely with many pastors over the years. To this day, they're some of our best friends. I've "roasted" them at banquets, presented them with fictitious awards, and played too many practical jokes on them to ever keep track of. I've also been the recipient of plenty of their practical jokes. Through it all, there's one thing I've discovered—most ministers have a terrific sense of humor.

If you don't already have a personal relationship with your pastor, get to know him or her today. I'm almost certain you'll find that in addition to being someone you can confide in, your pastor is someone you can have fun with, too. Being a pastor is hard work. There are all sorts of difficult situations with which a pastor must deal. Paul tells us in Hebrews that God will remember the things we do for our ministers. Adding laughter to their day is just one way we can help.

I would caution, however, against pulling pranks or practical jokes on any pastors before you've established a really good relationship with them and you know beyond a shadow of a doubt that their sense of humor can tolerate it. After all, pastors have access to church directories. They know where you live.

Thoughts to Ponder

What kind of relationship do you have with your pastor? Is it everything you'd like it to be?

Would you say your pastor is someone who enjoys laughter?

Bumper Sticker for the Day

Have you laughed with your pastor today?

Scripture to Stand On

For God is not unrighteous to forget your work and labour of love, which ye have shewed toward his name, in that ye have ministered to the saints, and do minister.

HEBREWS 6:10, KJV

Hello Again, Lord ...

Lord, thank you for those who you've placed over us. Help us to do everything we can to encourage them and lift their spirits whenever we can.

Eighteen
▲▼▲

Wah!

When was the last time you went to a restaurant and ordered off the kiddie menu? If a really cool toy came free with the meal, you might be tempted, but normally you'd order off the adult menu, wouldn't you? Puréed cheeseburger just doesn't sound that great, does it?

I'm sure you wouldn't ask for a high chair or a booster seat, either. You're too big for those things. Besides, the little plastic bib would probably cut off your airway.

Ever since you entered this world, you've been busy doing something—growing up. You've already passed through several stages of life, and in each stage you had different needs and desires.

When you were an infant, your parents never would have ordered you a steak or a charbroiled pork chop. Why? Well, for one thing, you didn't have any teeth. (You'll probably go back to that toothless grin in your senior years, but that's a long time away.)

Infancy is followed by the toddler years. As a toddler, you crawled around on the floor, putting everything in your mouth. (A two-year-old is the best vacuum around!)

Preadolescence came next. As a third-grader, I'm pretty sure you never brought a classmate home to your parents and announced your engagement.

Preadolescence was followed by the teen years. Now as a teenager, you're no doubt doing teenager things—listening to your stereo, talking on the phone with your friends, and if you have your license, you're trying your best to talk your parents into letting you borrow the car this Friday night.

Physical and emotional maturity comes in stages. Spiritual maturity does, too. Just as there are varying foods and actions suitable for our physical age groups, there are varying "foods" and actions suitable for our spiritual age groups, too. Paul tells us there is a time in our Christian walk when puréed spirituality and warm milk are the appropriate diet for us. They're easier for us to understand and digest.

Yet there comes a time when our spiritual appetites should be mature. We need the meat of the Scripture, not just the teething biscuits. We ought to be acting like spiritual teenagers and adults in our quest to know more of God, rather than still being in the nursery class, throwing tantrums and trying to have our own way instead of following God's.

Thoughts to Ponder
Think about your walk with the Lord. Would you say your spiritual age is appropriate, or is it time for you to grow up a little more?

Why do you think God wants us to develop a more mature spiritual appetite?

Bumper Sticker for the Day

> The Bible—food for all ages.

Scripture to Stand On
But solid food is for the mature, who by constant use have trained themselves to distinguish good from evil.

HEBREWS 5:14

Hello Again, Lord ...
Lord, when you're offering us steak, how can we stay satisfied with only the soup?

Nineteen

▲▼▲

Who Wants to Be More Than a Millionaire?

What if you were walking down the street and came upon a briefcase lying on the side of the road. Then, when curiosity got the best of you and you opened it, there inside was stack after stack of crisp, new one-hundred-dollar bills.

Your natural instincts would tell you that someone had lost it and needed it back, right? Well, what if you found a note inside that said, "Whoever finds this, please accept it as my gift."

Now what would you do? Would you walk away figuring it was some sort of trap? Would you take it and give it to someone else, saying, "I found this, but it can't be true. You take it and do whatever you want with it"?

Or would you keep it and go shopping?

God gave us the gift of salvation, through Jesus. It's free. He's left it in a place where we can easily find it—his Word. There's a note that basically says, "Whoever finds this, please accept it as my gift." Yet many of us walk away, figuring it can't be that easy. We may even show this gift to other people, but we walk away from it ourselves because we can't be fooled.

But if we leave it there, we are fooled. It's a free gift, far better than a briefcase full of one-hundred-dollar bills. It's a passage to peace, a ticket to eternal life with God. It's unearned love, unearned favor, and unearned redemption. And all we have to do is pick it up.

Thoughts to Ponder

Have you personally accepted God's free gift of salvation, or are you still walking by it, thinking it can't be as easy as it sounds?

Why do you think God made his salvation plan free, instead of something we have to earn?

Bumper Sticker for the Day

**Why does the best gift ever given remain
unopened by so many?**

Scripture to Stand On

How shall we escape if we ignore such a great salvation? This salvation, which was first announced by the Lord, was confirmed to us by those who heard him.

HEBREWS 2:3

Hello Again, Lord ...

Lord, thank you that your gifts don't come with an invoice.

Twenty
▲▼▲

Runaway

One afternoon while I was waiting outside a surf shop where my teenage son was shopping, a young man in his twenties approached my car.

"Do you have a file?" he asked, nervously looking over his shoulder at regular intervals. I thought this was a strange question until I noticed his right hand had handcuffs dangling from it. Needless to say, my heart started pounding.

Somehow I managed to get out the word, "No," while quickly rolling my window up, and, thankfully, he walked away. As soon as he was out of sight, I went inside the store and told the clerk what had happened, and he called the police.

Within minutes the police arrived, and they found the young man about two blocks away. I don't know why he was in handcuffs in the first place, but it was pretty certain that he was running from something.

Many of us are running, too, but it's a lot harder to see our handcuffs. We hide them, disguise them, or pretend they're not there, but they are there, whether we want to admit it or not. We're handcuffed to habits we'd like to break, people we know aren't good influences on us, and who knows what else?

There is hope. We can quit running. We just have to go to the right source and ask for the right help.

Thoughts to Ponder

Do you feel as though you're handcuffed to something and can't break free?

Have you gone to the right place for help? Have you asked Jesus?

Bumper Sticker for the Day

When you run, make sure it's in the right direction.

Scripture to Stand On

We have been made holy through the sacrifice of the body of Jesus Christ once for all.

HEBREWS 10:10

Hello Again, Lord ...

Lord, when I feel like running, may it always be to you.

Twenty-One
▲▼▲

Tunnel Vision

How would you like to live in a tunnel? Sure, it might be fun for a while. It'd be dark, so you'd hardly ever have to clean your room. And since you wouldn't know whether it was morning or night, you could sleep in as long as you like.

Still, there'd be a few drawbacks. For one thing, where would you plug in your computer? And while bats make interesting pets, they're probably not that good at playing Frisbee.

Tunnels don't give a realistic view of life, either. When you're inside a tunnel, all you know about is what's going on inside that tunnel and how it affects your own existence. The world above you could be at war or at peace, celebrating or rioting, and you wouldn't know the difference.

Some of us have chosen to live our lives not in a tunnel, but certainly with tunnel vision. We're only focused on what's happening within the confines of our own world, our own tunnel of self-concern. By doing so, we miss everything that's going on around us, the good times as well as the bad, the celebrations as well as the wars.

Tunnel vision is no way to view the world, because it records only what's right in front of it—your own life. But there's so much more to one's existence than that. Life is about interacting with others. It's about cherishing friends and coping with enemies. It's about loving and being loved.

View the world with tunnel vision and you'll miss out on an awful lot of the scenery.

Thoughts to Ponder

Would you say you have tunnel vision or peripheral vision when it comes to your view of life?

Why do you think it's harmful to focus on only your own life?

Bumper Sticker for the Day

Self-pity makes lousy company.

Scripture to Stand On

Let us not give up meeting together, as some are in the habit of doing, but let us encourage one another—and all the more as you see the Day approaching.

HEBREWS 10:25

Hello Again, Lord ...

Lord, I know I was never meant to be alone in this world. May I always invite others to join me in celebrating your gift of life.

Twenty-Two
▲▼▲

O Come All Ye Faithful

The book of Hebrews talks a lot about faith. Especially chapter 11. Chapter 11 tells us that by faith we can know God created the world. By faith Enoch was translated and did not face death. By faith Noah built an ark and was able to save his household from the great flood. By faith Sarah, a woman who should have been having a retirement party instead of a baby shower, bore a son, the fulfillment of a longstanding promise from God. And by faith Moses was able to pass through the Red Sea on dry ground.

God also tells us in that chapter that without faith, it's impossible to please him. So, what, then, is faith?

Faith is believing beyond a shadow of a doubt when man's reasoning points out all the doubts.

Faith is knowledge learned by the heart.

Faith is walking confidently to a place you've never been before, but knowing each step is sure.

Faith is hearing God's will louder than man's scoffing.

Faith is accepting the simplicity of the gospel without trying to complicate it.

Faith is putting your trust in God's power instead of man's limitations.

Faith is knowing there's more to life than what your human eyes are showing you.

Faith is surrendering your doubts and receiving all the reassurance you need.

Faith is the sense you believe with.

Thoughts to Ponder

Why do you think God said that without faith it is impossible to please him?

In what areas do you feel you need to have more faith?

Bumper Sticker for the Day

What does the Christian life and my cooking have in common?
They both require a lot of faith.

Scripture to Stand On

Now faith is being sure of what we hope for and certain of what we do not see.

HEBREWS 11:1

Hello Again, Lord ...

I know that faith is what it's all about, Lord. Help mine to grow more and more each day.

Twenty-Three
▲▼▲

The Real Story

People tell me I have this awful habit of letting them talk just so long about someone before I cut them off mid-tale with a sad story about whomever it was they were talking about. The story I tell is always true, and it usually makes the talebearer feel horribly guilty. The process goes something like this:

"Sheila is such a loser," someone will begin. "Can you believe that Saturday night she came to youth group totally stoned? She's doing drugs, I'm sure of it."

"You didn't hear?"

"Hear what? Did she get arrested?"

"No. She's on medication for a brain tumor. They discovered it because she's been losing her equilibrium lately."

"Uh ... well ... uh," the person will stammer. "A brain tumor?"

I nod as his or her face drops.

"Uh, I, uh, had no idea."

I fill in a few more details, then comes their disclaimer.

"Well, I knew she wasn't acting herself lately. That's why I said that. I mean, Sheila is usually so together and all. I certainly didn't mean to imply she was taking anything illegal."

At that point, the person's compassion and embarrassment is genuine. He or she feels horrible for having prejudged someone like that. Then the subject changes, quicker than a politician's promise after an election.

If we could train ourselves to think about what someone might be going through before we poke fun at, gossip about, or criticize that person, we'd save ourselves a lot of embarrassment. We could also save some hurting people a lot of pain.

Thoughts to Ponder

Have you ever teased or gossiped about someone, only to find out later that person was going through something you didn't know about? How did it make you feel?

Has anyone ever teased or gossiped about you without knowing the full story? How did it make you feel?

Bumper Sticker for the Day

When God promised us rest, that included our tongues.

Scripture to Stand On

Sometimes you were publicly exposed to insult and persecution; at other times you stood side by side with those who were so treated.

HEBREWS 10:33

Hello Again, Lord ...

Lord, remind me to think about the words that I speak, preferably before I speak them.

Twenty-Four

▲▼▲

It's Raining, It's Pouring

It's been responsible for terrible disasters. Cars have been washed away in it, houses have collapsed under its pressure, and at one time it even covered the entire world. What is it?

Rain.

Rain can do a lot of damage, can't it? It also does a lot of good. It can help extinguish a raging fire, make flowers grow, and fill up our rivers so we're not jet skiing on dirt. The remarkable thing about rain is it can do so much good and so much bad, but either way it still just comes one drop at a time.

So do words. Whether they're discouraging or encouraging, they come one at a time, and they can do a lot of good or they can cause a lot of destruction.

Let's face it. We all need encouragement to survive. Yet an accumulation of discouraging words can overtake us like a flood. So build a protective dam against them and don't let them drown your joy.

But when it comes to encouraging words, be a rain catcher. Save every single one of them, write them down in a journal, and remember them.

Thoughts to Ponder

Have you been saving the encouraging words that people or the Word of God have given you, or have you left yourself standing in a downpour of discouraging words?

Why do you think it's important to save the encouraging words that come your way?

Bumper Sticker for the Day

No one ever drowned in a sea of encouragement.

Scripture to Stand On

But encourage one another daily, as long as it is called Today, so that none of you may be hardened by sin's deceitfulness.

HEBREWS 3:13

Hello Again, Lord ...

Lord, I may not always have control over the words I hear, but help me to remember I do have control over the ones I save.

Twenty-Five

▲▼▲

Learning to Walk

When I run into people who knew me in high school, they usually say the same thing—"You haven't changed a bit." They're referring to physical changes, of course, and maybe to them it seems as though I haven't changed very much. I have basically the same hairstyle, wear the same size dress, and have the same sense of humor I had when I was a teenager. I would hope, though, that on the inside I'm different.

Each of us should be changing daily. We should be improving, learning, becoming more like the person God intended for us to be.

Take a moment to ask yourself a few questions.

Can your friends see growth in you or are you displaying the same immaturity in certain areas of your life that you displayed when you were in the fourth grade?

Do your parents see you throwing the same "tantrums" you did when you were a toddler, only instead of them being over a broken toy, they're now over whether you get to go to that unchaperoned party Friday night or buy that dress you can't afford or whatever else it is you're wanting to do that might not be in your overall best interest?

Do you actively try to pursue your career or life dreams, or do you just sit and whine, "Are we there yet?" without doing anything to help you get to your destination?

On the surface "you haven't changed a bit" sounds like a compliment. Yet, it can also mean you haven't improved or made any significant growth. It can mean that you're still crawling toward accomplishing that which you were meant to accomplish. Maybe it's time to stand up and walk.

Thoughts to Ponder

When you think over the past year, in what way would you say you have grown?

What changes do you think your family and friends can see in you? Are they positive changes or negative ones?

Bumper Sticker for the Day

Maturity=actions, not age.

Scripture to Stand On

For every one that useth milk *is* unskilful in the word of righteousness: for he is a babe.

HEBREWS 5:13, KJV

Hello Again, Lord ...

Lord, help me to have childlike faith, but not to stunt my spiritual growth with childish desires.

Twenty-Six

▲▼▲

Mud Bath

One of my favorite photographs is of my three sons covered in mud from head to toe. They were preschool age, and I captured the moment while they were playing in a mud puddle in our backyard.

Do you remember playing in mud puddles when you were a youngster? Fun, wasn't it? That is, until the mud got in your eyes or it started to dry and pinch your skin.

Or maybe you were minding your own business when you slipped in a mud puddle, and you weren't very happy about it.

No matter how we end up in a mud puddle, no matter how messy it is, or how dirty it makes us appear at the moment, the fact of the matter is, it's not permanent. Why? Because as soon as someone hoses us down or wipes us with a wet cloth, it all comes off. The thought of having to wear that mud for the rest of our lives never even crosses our minds, does it? No matter how much we get on us, we're confident it's all going to come off. We know mud isn't permanent. Regardless of how long we've been covered in it, it simply can't become part of our skin.

If you're still wearing some mud you got from slipping in one of life's mud puddles, or even playing in one, and you think it's never going to come off, think again. It's mud. Only mud. And it'll come off, every last speck of it, as soon as you ask God to shower you with his forgiveness.

Thoughts to Ponder

Are you still wearing some mud on you that you've convinced yourself is permanent?

Why do you think you've been choosing to wear it rather than let it be washed off and sent down the drain, where it belongs?

Bumper Sticker for the Day

> The only way to drown in a mud puddle
> is to lie face down in it and refuse to get up.

Scripture to Stand On

But when this priest had offered for all time one sacrifice for sins, he sat down at the right hand of God.

HEBREWS 10:12

Hello Again, Lord ...

Lord, thank you that not one of my failures is permanent.

Twenty-Seven
▲▼▲

A Neat Little Package

Wouldn't it be great if life came wrapped in one neat little package, gift-wrapped in beautiful paper, encircled with a ribbon and complete with a giant bow on top?

In case you haven't noticed already, it doesn't. The paper is prone to tearing, the ribbon can come loose, the bow doesn't always stick, and the tissue often starts peeking out of the box. In other words, life is far from neat and tidy.

We wish that weren't the case, don't we? We'd prefer all of our problems to have simple answers. We'd like people to live up to our high expectations of them, rather than letting us down time and time again. We'd prefer our days to be worry-free and all of our desserts to be calorie-free. We want that neat little package. Yet, all too often we get people who do let us down, we run into problems we didn't see coming, and we seem to gain weight from just walking down the Hostess aisle at the grocery market.

That's life. So, how can we cope with all that life throws at us? By lowering our expectations of a perfect life and raising our realization that even though things aren't perfect, we can deal with them. If the wrapping paper tears, God can help us tape it back together. If the ribbon comes undone, all we have to do is retie the knot. If the bow comes off or if we see tissue peeking out of the box, it's not the end of the world. After all, no matter what condition our wrapping is in, what's inside is still a gift, a gift to be cherished.

Thoughts to Ponder

Have you felt your wrapping coming undone lately?

What do you think God would say about the gift that is still inside of you?

Bumper Sticker for the Day

When the wrapping tears, don't toss out the gift.
Open it and enjoy.

Scripture to Stand On

But we are not of those who shrink back and are destroyed, but of those who believe and are saved.

HEBREWS 10:39

Hello Again, Lord ...

Lord, life isn't easy, but coming to you for help always is.

Twenty-Eight
▲▼▲

Just One More Thing ...

Have you ever wanted God to do something to prove he loved you? If he really loved you, that cute girl in science class would leave a note on your locker. If he really loved you, that boy would pay more attention to you. If he loved you, he'd help you with that English test—you know, that one you've had three weeks to study for but haven't gotten around to yet. If he loved you, he'd heal your grandfather of cancer, make your parents stop their fighting, and help you sell enough chocolate bars to win that new skateboard. If he loved you, he'd work out some way for you to get those $100 shoes you've been dreaming about. And so on, and so on, and so on.

Those things don't prove God's love for us any more than our going to church proves our love for him. Our bodies might be there, but our hearts and minds could be a thousand miles away.

God proved his love for us once and for all when he allowed his Son to die on the cross. That was the ultimate proof. If he never does another thing for us, if he doesn't answer another prayer, or give us another blessing, he loves us. If we doubt that fact, then we do not fully understand his sacrifice.

So, whether or not that cute girl or boy leaves you a note, whether or not you pass English class, your grandfather gets well, or your parents start getting along, none of that changes the fact that God loves you. He allowed his Son to die an excruciating death in our place to prove that fact. That's enough. All other blessings are simply a bonus.

Thoughts to Ponder

Have you ever wanted God to keep proving that he loves you?

Why do you think it's selfish of us to doubt his love?

Bumper Sticker for the Day

Do I love you?
Read my nailprints.
...Jesus

Scripture to Stand On

But we see Jesus, who was made a little lower than the angels, now crowned with glory and honor because he suffered death, so that by the grace of God he might taste death for everyone.

HEBREWS 2:9

Hello Again, Lord ...

Lord, forgive me for ever doubting your love.

Twenty-Nine

▲▼▲

Desperately Seeking Answers

On the way home today I passed a stretch limousine that was owned by a psychic. I knew that because of all the advertising on the side of the car. Business must be good.

Just this morning I received a telephone solicitation from a psychic hotline. It woke me up from a sound sleep. If the caller truly had had psychic powers, she would have known I didn't want to be bothered.

The truth is, people are seeking answers to the questions in their lives. They want to know what the future holds. They want to know whether the relationship they're in is going to last. They want to know who's going to win the Super Bowl. And they want to know if they're going to live a long life or drop dead in their tracks when they get their hotline bill. People have a lot of questions.

Yet, psychics aren't the place to look for real answers, answers that you can bank on. At $9.95 a minute, they'll bank on them, but you can't. So, if you really want to know what the future holds, the place you need to look is the Bible. Revelation will tell you all about the future. Proverbs can give you advice on your relationships. And if you want to know who's going to win the Super Bowl, there are at least a couple of teams even mentioned in the Bible—the Rams and the Bears. The Bible has it all.

If you're searching for real answers, make sure you go to the right place—God's Word. It's full of good news and it won't show up on your phone bill.

Thoughts to Ponder

Have you ever wished you knew what the future held for you?

Why do you think the Bible is the best place to look for answers?

Bumper Sticker for the Day

> The Bible—the hotline for your future.

Scripture to Stand On

Through Jesus, therefore, let us continually offer to God a sacrifice of praise—the fruit of lips that confess his name.

HEBREWS 13:15

Hello Again, Lord ...

Lord, when I have questions, thank you for having the answers.

Thirty

▲▼▲

Life's Driving Test

When we've made a wrong turn, why is "reverse" such a hard gear to find?

When the road gets a little rough, why do we start looking for the nearest off-ramp?

Why do we go so slow when it's time to forgive and go fast when it's time to condemn?

Why do we so seldom consult God's road map?

Why do we press the pedal to the metal at times when we should be applying the brakes?

Why do we apply the brakes at times when we should be pressing the pedal to the metal?

Why don't we notice when we're heading straight for a dead end?

Why do we shift to "park" when we should still be in "drive"?

Why do we so often cut off other people in our zeal to get to our destination?

Why do we use our horns more than our brains?

Why do we forget to thank those who have taken the time from their own journey to let us onto the road?

Why do we ignore the warning signs on our dashboard?

Why do we refuse to stop and ask directions?

Why do we inadvertently run so many people off the road?

Why do we allow ourselves to run so low on fuel?

When we see a fellow driver stranded by the side of the road, why don't we stop?

Why don't we realize getting a ticket from time to time could ultimately save our life?

Knowing the importance of arriving at our destination, why aren't we better drivers than we are?

Thoughts to Ponder

How do you think you would do on a driving test of life?

What can you do today to start brushing up on life driving skills?

Bumper Sticker for the Day

> Want to be a better driver in life?
> Attend God's traffic school.

Scripture to Stand On

That is why I was angry with that generation, and I said, "Their hearts are always going astray, and they have not known my ways."

HEBREWS 3:10

Hello Again, Lord ...

Lord, forgive me for the times when, in my hurry, I've driven right past your will for my life.

Thirty-One
▲▼▲

Speech Class

If someone asks forgiveness for stealing from us, the Bible tells us to forgive that person. It doesn't tell us that we're then obligated to make him or her our personal accountant. God expects us to use wisdom. Turning the other cheek doesn't mean standing there feeling helpless while someone emotionally beats you to a pulp. It means standing there with the power to retaliate, the right to retaliate, and choosing not to do so.

When Jesus remained silent at his trial, it was because he knew his silence was in God's plan. If it weren't, do you think anyone could have laid a finger on him? Before his arrest, whenever his accusers tried to trap him, Jesus either confronted them with Scripture, nullifying their accusations, as he did with the Pharisees, or he simply slipped away peacefully to continue with his ministry. Jesus knew when to speak and when to remain silent. He was meek, not weak. We often confuse the two.

If someone is continually hurting or bullying us, we sometimes think that if we refrain from speaking up for ourselves, we're being Christlike. Yet being Christlike means acting like Christ, both in our silence and when we speak up.

When you read the Bible, you'll see there are plenty of instances when it was in God's plan for his servants to be strong, to stand up to bullies, as when David stood up to Goliath or Gideon took on the bullying Midianite army with only three hundred soldiers.

How can we know whether God wants us to stand up or remain silent? By examining our hearts. If our silence in a confrontational situation is coming out of fear of speaking up, it's not meekness. It's weakness. If it's coming from prayerful restraint, then it's the right kind of silence. When the time comes, if we pray for God to help us, we'll know the difference.

Thoughts to Ponder

Do you think you've ever mistaken weakness for meekness?

Is there a situation in your life right now where you feel God wants you to hold your strength in check? Is there a situation where you think he might want you to stand up and show strength in him?

Bumper Sticker for the Day

> The best revenge is the one you're entitled to,
> but choose not to claim.

Scripture to Stand On

For we know him that hath said, Vengeance *belongeth* unto me, I will recompense, saith the Lord. And again, The Lord shall judge his people.

HEBREWS 10:30, KJV

Hello Again, Lord ...

Lord, when it comes to dealing with bullies, help me to know when I need to be an action drama or a silent movie.

Thirty-Two

▲▼▲

Who's the Boss?

Have you ever wanted to complain about a product or service, but didn't know who was in charge? Perhaps you even tried to get someone to direct you to the manager, the supervisor, or the CEO, but no one knew where they were, or even who they were. Frustrating, isn't it?

We don't have that problem when it comes to issues of this life. The Bible tells us plainly who's ultimately in charge. Of everything. That's "Everything" with a capital "E." Every single thing in this world and beyond is subject to him. Everything, past, present, and future. Everything. There's no question about it. Whatever our needs are, whatever our problems are, he's the one we ought to be talking things over with. His Word is the final word. He's the boss.

Realizing God is the boss, however, doesn't mean we're always going to understand his ways. Why, for example, would he choose to take kind, loving people home to heaven prematurely while difficult people seem to be blessed with long and healthy lives? We may not always understand why he allows some of the inhumane things that happen almost daily here on earth. But then again, he probably doesn't understand why we allow them to happen, either.

Whether we understand God's ways or not, there's still no escaping the fact that he's the final authority. He can do whatever he pleases. Luckily for us, he's a good God and has our best interests in mind 100 percent of the time. It's simply against his nature to do anything that would harm our eternal souls.

So, the next time you want to complain about something or ask one of those deep life questions, take it to God. If you really want the answer, he's the one you need to be talking to. And who knows, after seeing things from his perspective you might gain a new understanding of the situation. You might start learning to trust his judgment in more events in your life. And even if it's difficult to see it now, one day you may look back on your life and agree with every one of his decisions.

Thoughts to Ponder

Has God ever allowed something to happen in your life with which you disagreed?

Even though God might not have caused the event to happen, can you see any good that could one day come out of it?

Bumper Sticker for the Day

> Every good gift is from God.
> Where's your thank you note?

Scripture to Stand On

In putting everything under him, God left nothing that is not subject to him.

HEBREWS 2:8

Hello Again, Lord ...

Lord, thank you not only for being in charge of this world, but for being easily accessible, too.

Thirty-Three

▲▼▲

Prove It

Did you know love involves sacrifice? Anyone can say they love. They can sign it on the notes they write or say it just before they hang up the telephone. But the proof of their love isn't in their signature or in the words they speak. It's in what they're willing to sacrifice for that love.

Real love costs us something. It can cost us our sleep. Ask any mom or dad who has lain awake at night waiting for a teenager to arrive home safely. It can cost us time, money, food, and plenty more. Jack London once wrote, "A bone to a dog is not charity. Charity is the bone shared with the dog when you are just as hungry as the dog."

That's sacrificial love.

Jesus gave us the ultimate example of sacrificial love. Not only did he tell us that he loved us, but he was willing to lay down his life to prove it.

Remember, though, that Jesus didn't sin in his sacrifice. If a boy, girl, man, or woman asks you to prove your love for him or her by doing something that God wouldn't approve of, you won't be proving your love if you do it. You'll only be proving your own insecurities and your fear of losing that person's love. That's not sacrificial love. It's unhealthy love. Proving your love isn't something you have to do for people. It's something you choose to do.

Real love is volunteering to sell your ticket to Friday night's concert, because you'd rather spend the evening with your sister who's having a bad day. It's sharing your lunch with a friend who forgot his lunch money, instead of teaching him a lesson about responsibility while you eat two bologna sandwiches in front of him. It's being willing to make sacrifices when no one's asking you to do it, and no one's expecting you to do it, but you're doing it anyway.

It's called sacrificial love. It's God's kind of love.

Thoughts to Ponder

Has anyone ever asked you to do something God wouldn't approve of to prove your love? Why do you think that person was wrong in asking you to prove your love that way?

Have you ever voluntarily sacrificed something for someone else that you wanted yourself? Why do you think God was pleased with your sacrifice?

Bumper Sticker for the Day

Love without sacrifice doesn't suffice.

Scripture to Stand On

Let us fix our eyes on Jesus, the author and perfecter of our faith, who for the joy set before him endured the cross, scorning its shame, and sat down at the right hand of the throne of God.

HEBREWS 12:2

Hello Again, Lord ...

Lord, thank you for loving me with unselfish love.

Thirty-Four
▲▼▲

Follow the Leader

Remember when you were young and would play "Follow the Leader"? It was fun, wasn't it? You did everything exactly as the leader did it. You knew he or she wasn't going to march off a cliff and expect you to follow. The leader might get you to do something silly or embarrassing, but it was usually just good fun.

God has given us leaders to follow. Parents, pastors, teachers, principals, law enforcement officers, political officials—these are just some of the leaders we have today. Now, there may be a few bad apples in the bunch, but most of them can be trusted to have our best interests at heart. The rules they enforce are, more often than not, for our own good. We might not always agree with these rules, but unless they go contrary to the Word of God or are harmful to us in some way, we need to follow them. Why? Because these people have been placed in authority over us, and God is going to hold them accountable.

Our parents, pastors, teachers, principals, police officers, and politicians all have to give an account of their tour of duty over us. If we fail, they have to know that they did everything possible to prevent that failure. If we make wrong decisions, they have to know that they warned us ahead of time. God gave us the freedom to choose between right and wrong, but he also gave us helpers to guide us in making the right choices. Paul tells us that we should obey our leaders so that their work will be fun, instead of drudgery. If their work is fun, it stands to reason that we'll have a lot more fun, too.

Thoughts to Ponder

How does it make you feel to know that there are people who are going to have to give an account for you?

Do you feel you've been helping those in authority to do their job responsibly, or have you been hindering them?

Bumper Sticker for the Day

Life only gets tougher, the tougher we get.

Scripture to Stand On

Obey your leaders and submit to their authority. They keep watch over you as men who must give an account. Obey them so that their work will be a joy, not a burden, for that would be of no advantage to you.

HEBREWS 13:17

Hello Again, Lord ...

Lord, thank you for the authority figures in my life. Help me to do my part to make their job easier, so that they will be able to give you a good account one day.

Thirty-Five

▲▼▲

Field of Trampled Dreams

A bulldozer operator can drive over a field, see the flowers and weeds, and trample them both without giving any thought to the good he's destroying along with the bad. He leaves nothing in his wake but a field of flat, dry dirt.

A gardener, on the other hand, can walk through the same field, water the flowers, and pull at what weeds he sees, leaving a thing of beauty and possibility behind.

Some people are like bulldozer operators. When they discover someone else's faults, they begin driving over them with zeal, flattening each shortcoming into oblivion, without giving any thought to the good they might be destroying along with the bad. In their righteous enthusiasm to kill every weed, they sometimes destroy the flowers, too. Either they don't realize what they're doing or they simply don't care.

Others are like faithful gardeners. They see the weeds, but lovingly water the flowers first before gently tugging at what doesn't need to be there. With the right touch, most weeds give up without too much of a fight.

When we deal with the shortcomings of our friends, family, and even ourselves, we have the option to be either gardeners or bulldozer operators. It's up to us. We can destroy the good along with the bad, or we can be a little more careful and leave behind a thing of beauty that will continue to grow and flourish. Both a bulldozer operator and a gardener see weeds. Neither one are denying they're there. But the gardener sees the flowers, too, and does everything possible to protect them. The bulldozer operator just doesn't take the time.

Thoughts to Ponder

When you notice a friend's life becoming overgrown with weeds, would you say you're a bulldozer operator or a gardener?

When your own life is in need of a little weeding, which type of person do you respond to best—a bulldozer or a gardener? Why?

Bumper Sticker for the Day

Some of the prettiest flowers grow among the rocks.

Scripture to Stand On

Therefore, strengthen your feeble arms and weak knees.

HEBREWS 12:12

Hello Again, Lord ...

Lord, help me to not be so eager to change others to my liking that I destroy that which you want to protect.

Thirty-Six

▲▼▲

A Dash of Faith

Some recipes call for only a small amount of certain ingredients, yet these ingredients are vitally important. You don't need very much yeast to make bread, but without it, your nice fluffy loaf will be a cracker.

You only need a little bit of baking powder for cupcakes, but without it you might be baking hockey pucks instead of cupcakes. (I know. I've been supplying several hockey teams with their pucks for years.)

You might not need much chili powder in your enchilada sauce, but without that spice, your sauce would taste like tomato soup. Whether it's a cupful, a teaspoonful, or just a pinch, recipes need these important ingredients in order to turn out right.

The gospel needs a pinch of something, too—faith. The Bible tells us that if we have the faith of even a mustard seed, we could tell a mountain to cast itself in the sea and go surfing and it would. (Well, it doesn't say it in those exact words, but the message is the same.)

Some of us struggle with faith, though. We'll believe the gospel, we think, once we put all the pieces together in our mind, once we have every single one of our questions answered.

But that's not how it works. Faith is a necessary ingredient.

God could have presented the gospel to the world in a manner that didn't require any faith on our part, but he didn't. He chose to do it this way, to require something from us in return for all that he was offering. That requirement is faith.

Faith is a part of life. We have to have it in so many situations. Most of us don't have any trouble having faith in the pilot and the validity of his aviation school test scores every time we step onto an airplane. We exhibit faith in our hairstylist every time we sit down in his or her chair and say, "Just a trim, please." And I know my family has a lot of faith each evening when they sit down at the dinner table.

So for God to require a little faith on our part isn't really asking a lot, is it? Especially when he's giving us a whole lot more than a plane trip, a haircut, or my cooking.

Thoughts to Ponder

List three things in your everyday life that require faith on your part.

Why do you think God wanted to make faith a necessary ingredient to the gospel?

Bumper Sticker for the Day

Believe. It's not as hard as you think.

Scripture to Stand On

For we also have had the gospel preached to us, just as they did; but the message they heard was of no value to them, because those who heard did not combine it with faith.

HEBREWS 4:2

Hello Again, Lord ...

Lord, I believe in you. Not because all my questions are answered, but because all my emptiness is.

Thirty-Seven

▲▼▲

Wounded Warriors

Have you ever had someone tell you that they don't go to church anymore because of the hypocrites that are there? Or that they quit following God because of what a pastor, youth pastor, or certain deacon did?

Unfortunately, these stories of hypocrisy and misconduct are too often true. Pastors, youth pastors, deacons, choir directors, Sunday school teachers, and just ordinary Christians have been known to fall from grace, to talk one thing but walk another.

And yet, the behavior of the people who have let us down does not change one detail of what happened some two thousand years ago. The fact that the youth pastor gossiped about someone instead of praying for him or her doesn't for one second negate what Christ did on the cross. The fact that a pastor committed adultery doesn't mean that Jesus didn't live, die, and rise again.

As Christians, our behavior should reflect Christ's, but when it doesn't, Christ's behavior doesn't change. What he did for us on the cross isn't erased.

We're all human. We're going to slip up from time to time. We're going to let each other down. Yet when a fellow believer falls, it affects that person's spiritual walk, not the gospel. And just as we wouldn't want to be blamed for someone else's shortcomings, neither does the Lord. After all, he was perfect. And he's who we should be keeping our eyes on at all times anyway.

Thoughts to Ponder

Have you been let down by someone?

Have you responded to that person's need for grace and forgiveness in a way that you'd like others to respond to yours?

Bumper Sticker for the Day

The best way to break a fall is to fall on your knees.

Scripture to Stand On

See to it that no one misses the grace of God and that no bitter root grows up to cause trouble and defile many.

HEBREWS 12:15

Hello Again, Lord ...

Lord, forgive me when I'm having trouble forgiving others.

Thirty-Eight

▲▼▲

The Weather Report

There's a saying in Tennessee, "If you don't like the weather, wait an hour and it'll change." Clouds move fast here. It can be pouring down rain one minute and then there will be clear skies the next. Storm clouds gather, dump their fury, break up, and move on. Bad weather doesn't stick around. It changes. In fact, the weather changes no matter what part of the country you happen to live in. That's how God intended it. The rain comes, then it goes. Sunshine comes, then it goes. That's why weathermen aren't still talking about Hurricane Andrew or Hugo, nor are they still giving us a county-by-county report on a past tornado outbreak in Arkansas. Why? Because that weather occurrence is over. It has passed. There may be more hurricanes, floods, and tornadoes this year, but last year's weather isn't coming back. Change—that's what weather does. That's how God designed it.

Life is about change, too. Whatever storms we may have to endure today won't be hanging around very long, either. They may seem like they're never going to go away when we're in the middle of the downpour, but they will. We may have different clouds to face tomorrow, but the ones we're seeing today will pass on through. They always do.

So, whether your life's forecast is looking sunny or grim, the reality is, it's going to be a different scene tomorrow. Tomorrow could bring sunshine, or it could bring another cloudburst. Whatever it brings, though, we can get through it with God's help. Just like we do the storms that Doppler radar picks up. We'll get through them and talk about them for years to come, and each storm we survive will help us to appreciate the sunshine even more.

Thoughts to Ponder
Do you feel like you're in the middle of a downpour right now?

Think of a recent severe rainstorm. No matter how bad it looked at the time, did the sun eventually break through?

Bumper Sticker for the Day

> **Even Noah eventually saw an end to the storm.**

Scripture to Stand On
Land that drinks in the rain often falling on it and that produces a crop useful to those for whom it is farmed receives the blessing of God.

HEBREWS 6:7

Hello Again, Lord ...
Lord, when I'm in the middle of a downpour, help me to remember that your sun is still shining, even from behind the clouds.

Thirty-Nine

▲▼▲

Getting It Right

Jesus was born in a stable and gave himself for the world. Most of us were born in a hospital and think the world owes us something.

Jesus fed five thousand with five loaves and two fishes. We would've planned a potluck and still run out of food.

Jesus healed the sick. We ask "How are you?" then don't wait around long enough to hear the answer.

Jesus walked on water. We find it far easier to walk on each other.

Jesus said, "Peace. Be Still." We say, "Oh, my! Another storm! What'd I do to deserve this?!"

Jesus turned the water into wine. We turn molehill-sized problems into a mountain range of defeat.

Jesus raised the dead. Some of us go around so defeated that we look like the dead.

Jesus said, "Forsake not the little children to come unto me." We say, "Why didn't they leave that kid at home? I can't hear the sermon over all that crying."

Jesus prayed until drops of blood formed on his forehead. We pray until we figure the line is starting to form at the all-you-can-eat buffet.

Jesus was willing to lay down his life for us. We sometimes have a hard time laying down the remote for him.

Do you think we might be missing something?

Thoughts to Ponder

What else do you think we may be missing when it comes to following Christ's example?

Why do you think it's important to pattern our lives after the example that Christ gave to us?

Bumper Sticker for the Day

> When it comes to Jesus, it's OK to be a copycat.

Scripture to Stand On

This is the covenant I will make with them after that time, says the Lord. I will put my laws in their hearts, and I will write them on their minds.

HEBREWS 10:16

Hello Again, Lord ...

Lord, forgive us when we do things our way, instead of yours.

Forty

▲▼▲

We're Here Now

My husband hates it when plans change. If we walk into a restaurant that doesn't look as good on the inside as it did on the outside, instead of leaving, he'll say, "Well, we're here now, let's make the best of it." If we get on the wrong plane and end up in Greenland instead of Green Valley, California, he'll say, "We're here now. Let's make the best of it."

Just as restaurants and air travel sometimes let us down, life can deliver far less than we had hoped for, too. So, what do we do?

We say, "We're here now. Let's make the best of it."

The past is gone. Quit looking back. You can't erase that arrest record. You can't take back that experimentation with drugs or sex. You can't white out the F on the final. The important thing is, what are you going to do about it from this point on?

When the woman who was caught in adultery was brought to Jesus, he didn't deny the fact that she was caught in adultery. He didn't defend her sin. He didn't ask her why she did it. He was concerned with what she was going to do from that point on. He said, "Neither do I condemn you, go and sin no more" (Jn 8:11). He offered hope, not more condemnation. He was looking to her future, instead of dwelling on her past.

If you're in a place where you didn't expect to be, quit looking back. No matter what you've done, you're here now. Yesterday's gone. It's today. Make the best of it.

Thoughts to Ponder

Are you in a place right now where you didn't expect to be?

Why do you think God cares more about your future than about your past?

Bumper Sticker for the Day

If God had wanted us to keep looking back, he wouldn't have made it so uncomfortable on our necks.

Scripture to Stand On

For I will forgive their wickedness and will remember their sins no more.

HEBREWS 8:12

Hello Again, Lord ...

Lord, I can't change the past, but with your help, I can change my future.

Forty-One

▲▼▲

Truth Test

Too often, tragic stories of people with misplaced faith in a man or a cult have appeared in our news. We sit stunned in front of the television set, watching the aftermath of a mass suicide, and wonder how in the world thinking human beings could fall for such a baseless theology or belief system.

Paul warns us in Hebrews to beware of strange teachings. We're to test everything we hear against the Scriptures. If it's not in God's Word, we're to be leery of it. Better yet, we need to stay totally clear of it.

That's one of the main reasons to read your Bible. You need to know what it says. You need to know why it says what it says. You need to know God's promises, God's character, God's plan for your life, and God's plan for humanity. You need to know about the future and the end times. You need to know God's peace. You need to know his joy. You need to know his laws. You need to know his forgiveness. Then, when someone says something contrary to what is in the Bible, you'll be able to recognize it. When someone adds to the Scriptures, you'll know it. And when someone tries to minimize God's love for you, or the grace he's provided for you, or tries to twist his words in any way, you won't be fooled.

Thoughts to Ponder

Have you ever had to test a teaching against God's Word?

Why do you think Paul wants us to beware of teachings contrary to the Word of God?

Bumper Sticker for the Day

The Bible: the best fashion accessory.

Scripture to Stand On

Do not be carried away by all kinds of strange teachings. It is good for our hearts to be strengthened by grace, not by ceremonial foods, which are of no value to those who eat them.

HEBREWS 13:9

Hello Again, Lord ...

Lord, help me to be dedicated in studying your truth, and give me the wisdom to recognize it.

Forty-Two
▲▼▲

No Secret

Are you good at keeping a secret? When a friend confides in you about a certain situation, do you keep it in your heart and pray about it (providing his or her health or safety is not at risk), or do you publish it on your web page?

Hopefully, you're a friend who can be trusted with confidences.

I don't know how many times I've heard someone say "I'll tell you what she told me, but she told me not to tell anyone what she told me, so don't you tell anyone what she told me." In some bizarre way, people like this really think they're keeping the confidence by instructing everyone they tell to keep the confidence, too. In reality, the only thing they're doing is covering up the trail so the betrayal won't be traced back to them. When someone wants to tell us something that was told to them in confidence, we should walk away (and make a mental note that that's someone we probably won't want to confide in, in the future).

There is one secret, though, that we're not supposed to keep. That's the truth of God. God tells us over and over again to tell others about him. To pass along the stories of his goodness from generation to generation. To shout his praises. If we don't, then the rocks will, and that, I suppose, would be the ultimate rock concert. Jesus—he's one secret we're not supposed to keep.

Thoughts to Ponder

Why do you think God wants us to tell others about him?

If you had to write an introduction to God, what would you say?

Bumper Sticker for the Day

> If the gospel were a secret, would we spread it faster?

Scripture to Stand On

He says, "I will declare your name to my brothers; in the presence of the congregation I will sing your praises."

HEBREWS 2:12

Hello Again, Lord ...

Lord, your love is awesome, unconditional, amazing, and a lot of other things. But it's no secret.

Forty-Three

▲▼▲

Stickers

When I was growing up, my family and I used to take an annual cross-country vacation. I was the youngest of five children, so, counting our parents, there'd be seven of us piled into a midsize car, not counting all the luggage. On several trips, my siblings and I even managed to sneak our dog into the car and keep him quiet until we were a hundred miles or so into the journey. We figured if our parents discovered him at that point, we'd be too far along to turn back and take him home.

One of the things my parents enjoyed most about these trips, besides discovering the extra mouth to feed, was buying colorful stickers to glue on our car windows, attesting to all the different places we'd been. There was a sticker from the Grand Canyon, one from the Petrified Forest, and one from each of the states from California to Arkansas, and so on.

Whenever anyone noticed the stickers, my parents would proudly describe each place with a "been there, done that" sense of accomplishment. Every time we got a new car, I secretly figured it was because we needed more windows for all the stickers.

While those stickers documented plenty of good memories, I also have some that remind me of some not-so-good memories. "I survived the Northridge earthquake," says one. "I ate my own cooking and lived," says another.

Wouldn't it be great if people had life stickers that they could wear, telling about the kinds of "places" they'd been in their time on this earth? Without having to say a single word, we'd know about the blessings God had given them, as well as what trials they'd had to endure—the death of a parent, a divorce in the family, drug abuse, debilitating or life-threatening disease, low self-esteem, controlling parents, and so on.

Unfortunately, though, none of us come with life stickers. We just have to assume that each of us has had our share of both trials and blessings. No one's life is problem-free, nor is it without God's blessings. Life is like any journey. You're going to see some spectacular scenery, but you're probably going to have a few flat tires along the way, too. That's life. The journey is what you make it. Collect all the stickers you can.

Thoughts to Ponder

What kinds of joyous or hurtful "places" have you visited in your lifetime?

What important lessons have you learned through the hurtful places that you feel you could share with others?

Bumper Sticker for the Day

The real "survivors" are are the winners at life.

Scripture to Stand On

For the law made nothing perfect ... and a better hope is introduced, by which we draw near to God.

HEBREWS 7:19

Hello Again, Lord ...

Lord, I cherish the memories of all the places we've gone together.

Forty-Four

▲▼▲

Touched By a Pharisee

Have you ever been around people who execute God's judgment with perfect precision ... except when the rules apply to them? They're against divorce ... until their parents get one. They hold others to the letter of the law, while wrapping their sins in grace. The rules are black and white for everyone else, but shades of gray for them.

Sound like someone you know?

It sounds a lot like someone Jesus knew, too. The Pharisees. The Pharisees knew the law. They studied the law. They taught the law. Yet even they couldn't keep the law, not all of it anyway. That's why God had to send his Son to pay the price for our sins. None of us can be perfect. We can try, and we should, but too often we fail. We fail just like that person we enjoy monitoring fails.

If you have a Pharisee in your life, someone who judges you by the law, or his or her interpretation of it, instead of by mercy and God's interpretation of love, remember that Jesus had to deal with them, too. In fact, Jesus had more tolerance for the mistake-makers than he did for the perfection fakers.

We all need God's mercy and grace. All of us. Even Pharisees.

Thoughts to Ponder

If you had to convince God that your goodness was worth giving his son to die in your place, what would you say? Do you think that's enough?

Would you rather stand before God on the merits of your goodness or under the covering of his grace?

Bumper Sticker for the Day

Mercy—A Christian isn't fully dressed without it.

Scripture to Stand On

Day after day every priest stands and performs his religious duties; again and again he offers the same sacrifices, which can never take away sins.

HEBREWS 10:11

Hello Again, Lord ...

Lord, my own goodness will never be worthy of your sacrifice. Thank you for your love and mercy in spite of my shortcomings.

Forty-Five

▲▼▲

Halfway There

If you had tickets to your school football game on Friday night, would you get halfway there, pull over to the side of the road, and park? If you were invited to your friend's birthday party on Saturday, would you drive to within a block of the house, then turn around and go home? If you ordered a double dip hot fudge sundae with whipped cream, nuts, and a cherry on top, would you eat only the cherry and let the rest of it sit there and melt?

We usually don't do those kinds of things halfway, do we? When there's an event we really want to attend, or something we really want to do, we see it through to the end. We don't stop until we're where we want to be, or, as in the case of the hot fudge sundae, until we're licking the bottom of the dish and having major brain freeze.

God doesn't want us doing spiritual things halfway, either. Our reward, Paul tells us in Hebrews, is in completing the race, not getting to the halfway point then calling it quits. It's for those of us who stick it out to the end, who don't give up or give in, who refuse to let discouragement or interfering plans sidetrack us from completing our journey.

Halfway ... the only time it's a good idea is when you're eating my cooking. (It makes the stomach pumping go so much easier.)

Thoughts to Ponder

Would you say you tend to do spiritual things halfway?

Why do you think God wants us to know it's important to complete our journey with him?

Bumper Sticker for the Day

> If half is good enough, give your parents
> a 50 percent discount on your allowance.

Scripture to Stand On

Therefore, since the promise of entering his rest still stands, let us be careful that none of you be found to have fallen short of it.

HEBREWS 4:1

Hello Again, Lord ...

Lord, help me to remember that half way is never the best way when it comes to your ways.

Forty-Six
▲▼▲

No Download

Have you ever downloaded a file that took up most of your computer's memory? It's one thing when it turns out to be something you want, but when it doesn't, you can't hit the "delete" button fast enough, can you?

After all, why waste all that good memory on something you don't need? Or worse yet, on something that might contain a virus that could erase all your data. So you delete it, or you don't even download it in the first place.

Some of the things we're downloading in our life memory banks aren't worth all those megabytes either. That friend who betrayed us, that family member who said those cruel things to us, that youth pastor who was too busy to help us in our time of need—those are all things that can hog our memory banks until they finally rebel with "Sorry, there is not sufficient memory in your hard drive for this command." Worse yet, some of those bad memories might act like a computer virus that could threaten to shut down our entire system of peace and joy.

So, watch what you download into your mind. Every bad memory you hold onto takes up room that could be better used by something positive.

Thoughts to Ponder

Is there a bad memory that you'd like to replace with something better?

Why do you think it's not a good idea to use up all your memory space on useless clutter?

Bumper Sticker for the Day

> Good memories can be saved just as easily as bad ones can.

Scripture to Stand On

Consider him who endured such opposition from sinful men, so that you will not grow weary and lose heart.

HEBREWS 12:3

Hello Again, Lord ...

Lord, help me to save plenty of room in my memory bank for the good things you want me to remember.

Forty-Seven

▲▼▲

Dress Rehearsal

I've directed scores of plays and comedy sketches over the years, and one thing I've always been grateful for is the dress rehearsal. The dress rehearsal is where mistakes can happen—lines can be forgotten, stage lights may not work, costumes can need altering, a misprint may be discovered in the program, and the donkey carrying "Jesus" can decide to sit down in the middle of the aisle instead of walking down it.

That's OK, though, because it's only the dress rehearsal. It's not the real performance. You want the dress rehearsal to go perfectly, but if it doesn't, it's nothing to fret over. You just run through it again, and keep running through it until everything goes smoothly.

Unfortunately, life doesn't come with a dress rehearsal. This is it. We can't do it halfway, then take it more seriously the next time around. We get only this one chance. We have to make it count.

That's not to say we won't make mistakes. We will. But we should perform like it's opening night, give it our best shot, break a leg.

After all, once that curtain finally does come down and we take that final bow, we want a review to be proud of, don't we?

Thoughts to Ponder

Do you feel you're putting your best effort into making your life everything it can be for God?

If you had to write a review of your performance in life thus far, what would you say? As an "outside reviewer," what has impressed you? What has disappointed you?

Bumper Sticker for the Day

Your life's a play. Make every scene count.

Scripture to Stand On

We do not want you to become lazy, but to imitate those who through faith and patience inherit what has been promised.

HEBREWS 6:12

Hello Again, Lord ...

Lord, help me to remember that an obedient life will always get a standing ovation in heaven.

Forty-Eight
▲▼▲

The Right View

One night a lady was showing me some products from her Christmas store. When she came to one particular tapestry, I wondered what kind of sales pitch she was going to give it, because it was one of the most pathetic tapestries I had ever seen. Loose threads were sticking out all over and it didn't seem to form any pattern at all.

Yet that didn't stop the saleswoman in her.

"This would sell in a department store for three times this amount," she said, bubbling over with enthusiasm. "And it would look great in your house. It has all the right colors."

She continued her praise of the product, but the more she tried to convince me of its value, the less she seemed to believe in it herself. Her eyes seemed to be contradicting what she knew in her heart—it was the ugliest tapestry either of us had ever seen.

We both looked at it from all angles, trying our best to see why in the world the company would sell a product like this. Finally, she turned it over.

"Oh my goodness!" she laughed. "We've been looking at the wrong side!"

Once we turned it over, we could see that it was a beautiful tapestry indeed. Its beauty had been there all along. We just weren't looking at the right side.

Life has often been compared to a tapestry. We'll never see its beauty, either, if we spend all of our time looking at it from the wrong angle.

Thoughts to Ponder

Do you think you've been looking at life from the wrong angle lately, only seeing the loose threads and not the masterpiece it might become?

Take a few moments right now to try looking at it from a different perspective.

Bumper Sticker for the Day

> Even people with perfect vision don't always see correctly.

Scripture to Stand On

He also says, "In the beginning, O Lord, you laid the foundations of the earth, and the heavens are the work of your hands."

HEBREWS 1:10

Hello Again, Lord ...

Lord, thank you that even when all that I can see are the loose threads of my life, you're seeing the beauty of the completed tapestry.

Forty-Nine
▲▼▲

Making Faces

I heard a funny joke once about a little boy who was making ugly faces in class. Finally, his teacher told him, "If you keep making those ugly faces, Billy, your face will stay that way."

Billy looked at her, thought for a moment, then answered, "Well, Mrs. Johnson, you can't say you weren't warned."

Billy is, no doubt, still serving detention.

Just like Billy, we too have control over the faces we make, don't we? We can make happy faces, sad faces, angry faces, worried faces, shy faces, peaceful faces, puzzled faces, or any other kind of face we want. The expression we wear is totally up to us.

Why, then, do we keep letting our faces contradict us? We talk about being joyful while wearing sad faces. We tell others about God's peace while showing them our fearful faces. Our faces and our words are supposed to match. People should be able to see our joy, our peace, and our trust, not just hear us talking about it.

So, always wear a smile. Let the peace show through in your eyes. Make sure your face isn't saying one thing while you're saying another. Then, if Billy's teacher is right and our faces ever do freeze with one expression, at least it'll be one we can live with.

Thoughts to Ponder

Do you think your face matches your words?

Why do you feel it's important to let others see God through your expression, not just your words?

Bumper Sticker for the Day

Smile even when you don't feel like it.
The rest of you will eventually catch up.

Scripture to Stand On

You need to persevere so that when you have done the will of God, you will receive what he has promised.

HEBREWS 10:36

Hello Again, Lord ...

Lord, when I'm at peace, when my life is filled with joy, when I know who I am in you, please help me to remember to tell my face.

Fifty
▲▼▲

The Fights

My father used to watch boxing matches on television. He would sit in front of the television set for what in retrospect seemed like every night and watch two men beat each other to a pulp.

Even though boxing didn't hold much interest for me, I was still able to take something valuable away from that experience. First and foremost—writing is a much safer career choice than boxing. But I also saw that no matter how bloodied each man got, no matter how many blows to the head, gut, or chest he endured, no matter how often he went down for the count, no matter how many times they played the theme from *Rocky,* the only thing that truly mattered was which one of them was still standing at the end of the fight. The victor wasn't the one who had shed the least amount of blood, or had the fewest bruises, or had the most loyal and vocal fans encouraging him to "get back up!" The victor didn't have to have the best moves, the most muscle, or the coolest outfit. The victor was the one still standing at the end. It was as simple as that.

You may feel as though life has been giving you a series of one-two punches lately. You may think there's no way you can get up. You may be lying there face down on the canvas, and instead of the crowd cheering you on, all you may be able to hear is an arena of people telling you that you can't do it.

Yet listen a little closer. It's not hopeless. The referee is still counting. The final bell hasn't rung yet. The fight isn't over.

With God's help and your determination, you can, should, and hopefully (will) get up again.

Thoughts to Ponder

What kind of one-two punches have you been enduring lately?

Think of God as your manager. What do you think he is saying to you right now?

Bumper Sticker for the Day

> Many a fight has been won by someone who was, at one point, down for the count.

Scripture to Stand On

We want each of you to show this same diligence to the very end, in order to make your hope sure.

HEBREWS 6:11

Hello Again, Lord ...

Lord, help me to remember that falling facedown on the canvas won't cost me the fight. But laying there and surrendering will.

Fifty-One

▲▼▲

Wasted Time

Have you ever wasted time on someone or something that didn't deserve it? I'm not talking about someone's eternal soul. An eternal soul is always worth our time. I'm talking about difficult people or negative situations that aren't worth the time we spend fretting over them.

When we focus all our attention on those in our lives who aren't supportive, we take away time from those who are. When we dwell on the actions of those who merely love us to our face, we inadvertently take time and energy from those who love us from all angles.

The true power of an enemy isn't in what they take from us. It's in what we give them. And often what we give them is much more than they deserve. We give them time that could be better spent talking with the Lord, reading our Bible, enjoying the company of supportive friends and family members, or even just resting in the Lord. We also give them a good share of our peace and our joy.

We have only so much time allotted us here on earth. Even if we live to be a hundred years old, that's not a lot of time. So, don't allow negative people or ongoing negative situations to drain your time and energy. Pray for them, react to them in a godly manner, but use your energies on more important matters. Life is too precious to waste a minute of it.

Thoughts to Ponder

Would you say you spend more of your time and attention appreciating the positive people in your life or fretting over the difficult ones?

Why do you think God wants us to use our time and energy in more productive ways?

Bumper Sticker for the Day

Why does he who gave his all for us
get so little of us in return?

Scripture to Stand On

To which of the angels did God ever say, "Sit at my right hand until I make your enemies a footstool for your feet"?

HEBREWS 1:13

Hello Again, Lord ...

Lord, help me to keep my priorities straight and never move you out of the number-one position.

Fifty-Two
▲▼▲

Hit and Run

Have you ever had someone say something snide to you, then take off before you could answer, or at least ask what he or she meant by it? I'm pretty slow when it comes to rude comments. I tend to give people the benefit of the doubt, unless they've proven time and time again that their motive is to hurt. More often than not, though, I'm not expecting people to be rude. So when they are, it takes me by surprise. It doesn't dawn on me for weeks, months, sometimes even years, that someone has been rude. In fact, I just had a revelation the other day that a comment a sales clerk made to me back in '89 was probably intended to be rude. I've got a comeback for her now, but she probably doesn't work there anymore.

It's just as well. Rude comments don't need a comeback. You're better off ignoring most of them. People who "hit-and-run" are really just taking the easy way out. It doesn't take a lot of courage to scoff and take off. What takes courage is to stay and discuss an uncomfortable situation, a disagreement, or a misunderstanding.

So, if you've been the victim of a hit-and-run comment, remember rudeness reflects on the one displaying it, not on the recipient. Or maybe you're the one who's prone to sarcastic "hits." I'm not referring to good-natured joking, but "hits" that are intended to hurt. Would you say this is a fair way to get your point across, or would it be better to discuss the situation like an adult? A vehicular hit-and-run is illegal. A verbal hit and run is wrong, too.

Thoughts to Ponder

Can you think of a time when someone committed a verbal hit and run on you? How did it make you feel?

Can you think of a time when you might have committed a verbal hit and run on someone else? If you could relive that moment, what would you do differently?

Bumper Sticker for the Day

No one wins a debate where only one side does the talking.

Scripture to Stand On

Do not harden your hearts as you did in the rebellion, during the time of testing in the desert.

HEBREWS 3:8

Hello Again, Lord ...

Lord, help the words that come from my mouth always be pleasing to you, and help me to leave some room for others to talk, too.

Fifty-Three

▲▼▲

You Should Have Known Better

Why do we understand the concept of overlooking someone's faults before they come to Christ, but find it so difficult to do the same afterward? Jesus didn't tell us to take up his cross and be perfect. He said, "Take up my cross and follow me" (Mt 16:24). That means each one of us will be forever striving for perfection, but we won't attain it. We can't. At least not in this life. We'll make mistakes—minor ones and major ones—but we don't have to turn the cross in every time we stumble and fall. Jesus doesn't say, "You should have known better." He doesn't turn away from us and complain, "Why do I even bother?" He's ready to forgive 100 percent of the time.

I wish I could say we are, too. We have a more difficult time forgiving each other. Especially other Christians. It's just too hard to forgive that person who's been teaching Sunday school for ten years, or that minister or youth pastor who knew better than to get involved with this sin or that.

Yet that isn't how Jesus looked at our human failings. He didn't tell Peter, "Boy, did you ever let me down. You really blew it this time. I don't think I can ever forgive you." No. Jesus knew that even though Peter was a believer, he had human frailties. Jesus knew his heart and forgave him.

I was backstage at an awards ceremony once when the news had just broken about the moral failure of a well-known Christian artist. Someone asked Michael W. Smith if he'd heard about it and what he thought. You could tell his heart was broken for his friend, and he simply said, "There but by the grace of God go any of us."

His response impressed me. He didn't join what was sure to become a bandwagon of condemnation. He had a heart for a friend who was suffering because of bad choices. How many of us can say we're that kind of a friend to the fellow believers we know who fall?

Thoughts to Ponder

When you hear about a fellow believer who stumbles, what's your first reaction? Concern or ridicule?

Why do you think you should be following Christ's example in how you treat others who have stumbled?

Bumper Sticker for the Day

Wanna know who your real friends are?
Get to your lowest point, then look around.

Scripture to Stand On

For this reason he had to be made like his brothers in every way, in order that he might become a merciful and faithful high priest in service to God, and that he might make atonement for the sins of the people.

HEBREWS 2:17

Hello Again, Lord ...

Lord, you hate all sin, but being judgmental is on the top of your list. Help me to remember to be as merciful to others as I'd want you to be to me.

Fifty-Four

▲▼▲

Awesome

The late Rich Mullins wrote about our "awesome God." Our God *is* awesome, isn't he? As descriptive as that song is, however, it still doesn't capture the full essence of God. That's because the goodness and greatness of God defies description. How can anyone accurately describe a God who can speak one word and have the whole world come into existence? Think about how intricately everything is made—mankind, animals, plants, vegetables, the stars, the sun, the moon, the oceans, the weather. Each of these systems has systems within it, all working in concert with each other. Someone had to design all that. It didn't just happen.

How could anyone describe a God who loves so unselfishly that he would give his Son to die in the place of a people who had rebelled against him? That's an awesome God.

How can you describe his mercy, his justice, his power, his care, his grace, his plans, his glory, his forgiveness, his understanding, his wisdom? You can't. Seeing just a little glimpse of who he is, how does it feel to put your problems into the hands of a God like that? Doubting his power seems a little silly, doesn't it?

Thoughts to Ponder

How would you describe God?

Do you think most people underestimate God's greatness and goodness?

Bumper Sticker for the Day

An awesome God loves awesomely.

Scripture to Stand On

When God made his promise to Abraham, since there was no one greater for him to swear by, he swore by himself.

HEBREWS 6:13

Hello Again, Lord ...

Lord, thank you for perfectly loving an imperfect people.

Fifty-Five

▲▼▲

Holy Style

In my lifetime I've seen a lot of styles come and go. I remember the big hair era, which I understand is now making a comeback. (The best thing about big hair is that it makes a great cover to hide behind on oral report day.)

Then, there was the baggy pants era. Many parents didn't like this one, and I can understand their concern. It was too easy for teenagers to hide report cards, homework, junk food, and stray dogs under there.

Miniskirts have the opposite problem.

From cargo pants to skater jeans to spiked hair to no hair, styles come and go. Garments wear out, or we sell them at yard sales and go shopping for the next hot trend.

Yet God isn't a trend. He doesn't change his ways to suit our designer taste of the moment. He is who he is, regardless of who we're trying to be. He's constant and can be counted on to be around not just this fashion season, or the next one, or the one after that.

He's eternal, and his ways set the ultimate style. The world may say it's vogue to be self-serving. God says loving others more than yourself is in style. The world may say greed is the latest trend. God says an unselfish spirit is what's hot. The world may say disobedience and rebellion are what all the designers are recommending this season. God says to stand up for what's right even if it seems old-fashioned. Be a trend-setter. Follow God's style.

Thoughts to Ponder

Can you think of some styles that you've seen come and go in your lifetime?

Why do you think it's important to have a solid faith, one that doesn't change with the times?

Bumper Sticker for the Day

When you change your style, don't let your faith go with it.

Scripture to Stand On

They will perish, but you remain; they will all wear out like a garment. You will roll them up like a robe; like a garment they will be changed. But you remain the same, and your years will never end.

HEBREWS 1:11-12

Hello Again, Lord ...

Lord, thank you for your consistency in an ever-changing world.

Fifty-Six

▲▼▲

Predictable Unpredictability

Ever have one of those days when things seem to go from bad to worse? I had one recently. I was driving home with my daughter-in-law, Crystal, when it started to pour. I soon discovered that my car I was in desperate need of new windshield wipers. They were going back and forth, but instead of clearing off the windshield, they were just smearing it. There wasn't any gas station nearby, so we drove on, praying and hyperventilating and trying our best to see the lines of our lane through the rain and the darkness.

Of course, things got worse. The headlights from the oncoming cars bounced off the wet pavement and the blurry windshield, impairing visibility even more.

And things got worse still. The street on which I was driving was in the middle of reconstruction. The heat from the hot asphalt mixed with the cold air and formed a huge steam cloud, bringing visibility now down to almost zero.

And yes, things got even worse. As I approached the street where I needed to turn, I squinted, trying to see the curb through the cloud. But it wasn't there. Someone had moved it! In its place was a ten-foot mountain of dirt and a cement barricade, blocking entrance into my subdivision.

Outside of actually having an accident, I don't think things could have gotten any worse, but miraculously, we made it home safely. Life is unpredictable. On any given day, we don't know what circumstances we're going to find ourselves in, often without any warning. We don't know what dangers, inconveniences, blessings, aggravations, or good times are going to come our way. The only thing we can do is trust that God is in control and will be with us through all of it—our good days and even those days when things just keep going from bad to worse.

Thoughts to Ponder

Think of an unexpected crisis that came your way recently. Was there any way you could have known it was coming?

How does it make you feel to know that God can be counted on when little else can be?

Bumper Sticker for the Day

> Life is unpredictable.
> God's ability to help us through isn't.

Scripture to Stand On

Therefore, since we have a great high priest who has gone through the heavens, Jesus the Son of God, let us hold firmly to the faith we profess.

HEBREWS 4:14

Hello Again, Lord ...

Lord, thank you for being a God who can always be counted on.

Fifty-Seven

▲▼▲

Where'd Everybody Go?

Magicians and illusionists aren't the only ones who can "disappear." My family and friends disappear the minute I say, "Dinner is served." Some people disappear the minute it's time to do chores or their homework. And unfortunately, there are even some who disappear the minute someone needs them.

"Where'd they go?"

"I don't know. They were here just a minute ago."

When the going gets tough, some people have a real talent for disappearing into thin air.

I'm sure it hurt Jesus when those he had helped disappeared on him. All the people who had followed him from sermon to sermon, the five thousand he had fed, those he had healed, and of course, his disciples. These were twelve men who had traveled with him, knew his family, and knew firsthand that he wasn't a lunatic or a blasphemer. They had seen evidence of his deity, they had heard his message, and they had wholeheartedly, or so it had appeared, supported his mission. Yet, when it was going to cost them more than they expected, they stood by and didn't utter a single word in Christ's defense. When their friendship was most needed, they were no where to be found. Martin Luther King Jr. once said, "In the end, we will remember not the words of our enemies, but the silence of our friends."

Jesus forgave his friends because he loved them. But their disappearing act had to have hurt him. After all, in the face of accusation, ridicule, and whatever else may happen to come up, real friends don't let friends stand alone.

Thoughts to Ponder

Have you ever disappeared on a friend?

Why do you think it's important to be there for your friends even when it's difficult to do so?

Bumper Sticker for the Day

> **A true friend doesn't leave
> when the storms start to gather.**

Scripture to Stand On

For we do not have a high priest who is unable to sympathize with our weaknesses, but we have one who has been tempted in every way, just as we are—yet was without sin.

HEBREWS 4:15

Hello Again, Lord ...

Lord, when you're counting on my friendship, help me not to be a disappearing act.

Fifty-Eight

▲▼▲

A Sure Thing

I've long heard it said that the only two sure things in life are death and taxes. There may be a few other sure things, too. For instance:

It's a sure thing that the very instant you turn around to tell that boy behind you to quit kicking your chair, your teacher will look up and see you talking to him.

It's a sure thing that after leaving a tuna sandwich in your locker all weekend, Monday will be the day that cute guy (or girl) you've been wanting to meet all semester will have his (or her) locker reassigned next to yours.

It's a sure thing that the morning your little sister plays "beauty shop" with your face, drawing bright red clown lips and highlighting your cheeks with multicolored glitter, will be the one morning you forget to check yourself in the mirror before going to the mall.

It's a sure thing that the load of laundry already in process that you sneak your favorite white top into will contain a red sweater you don't see.

It's a sure thing that the minute you turn on the shower, others in your house will turn on the dishwasher, the washing machine, and the garden hose simultaneously.

It's a sure thing that eating my cooking will leave you spending the rest of the day in the doctor's office, moaning, "It was the liver muffin! It had to have been the liver muffin!"

These are just a few of the certainties we face in life. There are hundreds of others, I'm sure, but death and taxes still remain pretty high on the list. We don't have to fear them, though. Our vote helps us do something about taxes. And if we've made the best of our time here on earth, we don't have to fear death either. Now, as far as fearing my cooking goes? Well, that's a different story.

Thoughts to Ponder

What have you found to be a sure thing in your life?

Do you think you're making the best use of your time here on earth?

Bumper Sticker for the Day

> Time is like your allowance.
> Once spent, you can't get it back.

Scripture to Stand On

Man is destined to die once, and after that to face judgment.

HEBREWS 9:27

Hello Again, Lord ...

Lord, help me not to waste a single moment of my life. Help me to learn from the past, plan for the future, but live in the now. Today is the day that truly counts.

Fifty-Nine

▲▼▲

Postponed Lessons

One day while standing in line at Kinko's, waiting to pay for my purchases, the lady behind me tried to convince the clerk to let her slide on paying for her fax because all she had was a fifty-dollar bill. The clerk had already explained to the woman that if she would wait until he could get change, he'd help her. It wasn't even her turn in line anyway, but again she pressed, "Can't I just pay you next time?"

"Sorry," the clerk said. "I can't do that."

The woman was obviously upset. Finally, she looked around at the rest of us waiting patiently for our turn in line.

"Does anybody have a dollar?" she asked.

I don't know why I did it, but I found myself saying, "Sure, here," and handing her one of mine. I had met her impatience, not her need. The lady didn't really need my dollar. She was at Kinko's, not a food bank. And she had already let everyone in the place know that she had a much larger bill on her. She simply didn't want to have to wait her turn. Or wait at all, for that matter. She needed to learn patience, but I, without meaning to, got in the way of that lesson.

I know that, because when the woman took the dollar from my hand and handed it to the clerk, she slapped it down on the counter, saying, "Here!" as if my dollar somehow vindicated her. She was so focused on her "need" of the moment that she didn't even notice anyone else around her. She didn't care that the clerk was in a predicament and couldn't get change right at that moment or that a total stranger had just sacrificed her own dollar.

As I walked out of Kinko's, I couldn't help but ask myself how many other times I've gotten in the way of someone learning a lesson. Whether it's a lesson in patience, in trust, in generosity, or in self-sacrifice, if we step in too quickly to help, no one will learn anything from the situation. I'm not saying we should withhold good when it's in our power to help someone. We shouldn't. But we should also weigh the situation. If a person's safety or well-being isn't an issue, only their ego, patience, or greed, then maybe we shouldn't be so eager to step in. My gift helped that woman for the moment, but in the long run, it may have done her more damage than good.

Thoughts to Ponder

Have you ever gotten in the way of someone else's lesson?

Why do you think all of us have to sometimes learn lessons the hard way?

Bumper Sticker for the Day

> Those who always land on a pillow never learn
> that falling hurts.

Scripture to Stand On

Although he was a son, he learned obedience from what he suffered.

HEBREWS 5:8

Hello Again, Lord ...

Lord, give me the wisdom to discern when my actions help and when they hinder.

Sixty

▲▼▲

One of These Days

Are you a procrastinator? Do you put off cleaning your bedroom until the ants are having to march upright because there's no place to walk? Do you procrastinate changing your sheets until the floral pattern has taken root? Do you hold off taking out the trash until the piles are so high they're being listed on maps as a new mountain range?

How about your schoolwork? Do you procrastinate with that, too? Do you find yourself finishing that term paper on your way to class? Or studying for that exam while your teacher is passing out the test papers?

Do you put off diets? Exercise programs? Haircuts? Baths?

Do you procrastinate on letters you need to write, people you need to call, or promises you need to keep?

How about church? Do you put off joining the band? Participating in youth group? Fulfilling commitments you made to your pastor?

The Bible talks a lot about today. God's more concerned with what you do right now than with what you did yesterday or what you vow to do tomorrow.

In Hebrews, the Holy Spirit says, "Today, if you hear his voice." It doesn't say, "You should have heard his voice yesterday. Why weren't you paying attention?" Nor does it say, "Plan to hear his voice tomorrow. Go ahead and do what you want today, but you'd better be paying attention to him tomorrow!"

The Holy Spirit says to listen to God today. Don't procrastinate until tomorrow or beat yourself up over yesterday. This day is the most important day on the calendar. This hour. This moment. Treat it that way.

Thoughts to Ponder
Would you say you're a procrastinator?

Why do think God is more concerned with what you do right now than with what you did yesterday or will do tomorrow?

Bumper Sticker for the Day

When opportunity knocks, don't pretend you're not home.

Scripture to Stand On
So, as the Holy Spirit says: "Today, if you hear his voice..."

HEBREWS 3:7

Hello Again, Lord ...
Lord, thank you for the lessons of yesterday and the hope for tomorrow, but most importantly, thank you for the opportunities of today.

Sixty-One

▲▼▲

The Defense Doesn't Rest

Do you like watching court shows, such as "Law and Order," "The Practice," and "Judge Judy"? In court, the accused are always allowed an attorney. If they can't afford one, one will be assigned to them, unless they choose to represent themselves. Attorneys are good to have, especially in serious cases. They speak up for you when you can't or don't know how to speak up for yourself. They look out for you. They hold your reputation, freedom, and perhaps even your life in their hands, and if they're responsible, they don't take that assignment lightly.

The Bible tells us that Jesus is our attorney. He's the one who intercedes in our defense. He holds our freedom, reputations, and lives in his hands, and he's already proven on the cross that he doesn't take that assignment lightly.

Each one of us has already been charged with breaking God's laws. We could all easily cite the different infractions that are on our "rap sheet." It doesn't matter whether we have a short list, a long list, or one that makes Al Capone look like an altar boy, we all have a rap sheet.

But once we allow Jesus to be our attorney, he pleads our case for us. He tells the court of the good in us, instead of putting our crimes on the overhead projector for all to see. Even if the DNA is found to be a perfect match, and it will be, he reminds the court that the crimes we have committed have already been paid for. No matter how many witnesses the prosecution calls or how many times he stands and objects, with one mention of the word "grace," Jesus leaves the prosecution speechless. From a convincing opening argument to a powerful, flawless closing statement, Jesus not only proves our worth to the court, but our worth to him as well.

Eternity—don't face it without a good attorney.

Thoughts to Ponder

How does it feel to know that there is someone who is always defending the good in you?

Do you think you could defend your innocence to God if you had to do it without grace?

Bumper Sticker for the Day

The real "Dream Team"? The Father, Son, and Holy Ghost.

Scripture to Stand On

Therefore he is able to save completely those who come to God through him, because he always lives to intercede for them.

HEBREWS 7:25

Hello Again, Lord ...

Lord, thank you for always interceding on my behalf.

Sixty-Two

▲▼▲

Did You Say Something?

If you ignore it, it'll go away." Have you ever heard that phrase? It's usually spoken in reference to a problem of some sort. If you ignore it, they say, eventually it won't be a problem.

That's not always true, though. Some troubles only get bigger the more we ignore them. If you don't believe me, try ignoring an avalanche. It might be easy to pretend that first snowball didn't hit you on the head, but when the whole mountain is coming down on top of you, you might as well go ahead and acknowledge it.

Ignoring your conscience, though, will make it go away. A healthy conscience needs and demands your attention. Contrary to common belief, a conscience doesn't nag. It's not pushy. In fact, it's pretty sensitive. It'll give you just so many chances, and then its voice will begin to weaken and grow distant. It won't stay where it's not wanted. Continue to ignore it and it'll just slip away into the night without you even realizing it, much like my dinner guests.

So the next time your conscience speaks, listen to it. It wants to help you make the right decisions. It's on your side. And it usually knows what it's talking about.

Thoughts to Ponder

Do you feel your conscience is as strong today as it was six months ago?

Why do you feel it's important to pay attention to your conscience?

Bumper Sticker for the Day

> ...got conscience?

Scripture to Stand On

Pray for us. We are sure that we have a clear conscience and desire to live honorably in every way.

HEBREWS 13:18

Hello Again, Lord ...

Lord, help me to listen to my conscience when it speaks ... even if I have to turn down the other noises of life to hear it.

Sixty-Three

▲▼▲

The Pleasure of Your Company

If you had the option of taking someone along with you on a trip, who would you choose—a skeptic who thought he or she had already seen everything, knew everything, and was so familiar with the road you'd be taking that nothing excited him or her anymore, or someone who had childlike enthusiasm and awe, even though they were clueless about the road.

I don't know about you, but I'd rather be around people who are unsure of all the directions, but excited about the destination, people who are not afraid to admit they don't know everything, but trust the driver to show them the best scenery there is to see.

Sometimes I think those of us who don't have a clue about what we're doing are the ones God enjoys taking on adventures. We're more fun. It's not a lot of fun to give people something they expect to get or think they deserve. It's not fun to be with people who think they know the road so well that they tell you where you should turn at every crossroads. Especially when you're trying to show them an incredible view down to the right, but they keep on insisting you should turn left.

When we don't know what the future holds, when we trust God to map out our journey for our best enjoyment, when we get excited over the possibilities, instead of being bored at every turn, I think God just enjoys us more. And we enjoy the trip a lot more, too.

Thoughts to Ponder

Would you say that you're looking in awe at the places God is taking you?

Why do you think it's important not to lose your childlike enthusiasm for your life's journey?

Bumper Sticker for the Day

Even God enjoys good company.

Scripture to Stand On

Because God wanted to make the unchanging nature of his purpose very clear to the heirs of what was promised, he confirmed it with an oath.

HEBREWS 6:17

Hello Again, Lord ...

Lord, help me never to lose my childlike excitement in my journey through this life with you.

Sixty-Four

▲▼▲

Contentment, Not Resentment

Comedian Jeff Allen does a bit where he talks about the difference between our needs and our wants. We may want a hundred-dollar pair of athletic shoes, for example, but we don't usually need them. It's a very funny routine, and if you ever get the chance to see him in concert, I highly recommend it.

The Bible talks about the difference between our needs and wants, too. Paul tells us to be content with whatever we have. If we learn contentment, we can be happy whether we win a hundred dollars in that fast food giveaway or a large fries. If we learn contentment, we can be just as happy about getting selected to empty the classroom trashcan as we are about making the football team. If we learn contentment, our faith and joy are secure, no matter what our circumstances happen to be.

Contentment is an important quality to have as a Christian. If our faith and joy are tied to our financial status, our spirits will sink and our faith will crumble the minute our savings account balance drops too low. If our faith and joy are tied to our popularity, we'll lose both the first time we lose a school election. If our faith and joy are tied to anything other than God's love, we're on unstable ground.

That's why Paul tells us to be content with what we have. It's God who will never leave us or forsake us. Not Master Card. Not our savings account. Not that concert we want to attend on Friday night. Not superficial friends. Not fame. God. He's consistent and faithful. Be content.

Thoughts to Ponder
Is there a "want" that you've been confusing with a "need"?

How does it make you feel to know that God will never leave you, no matter what?

Bumper Sticker for the Day

God promises the desires of our hearts,
and he doesn't charge interest.

Scripture to Stand On
Keep your lives free from the love of money and be content with what you have, because God has said, "Never will I leave you; never will I forsake you."

HEBREWS 13:5

Hello Again, Lord ...
Lord, thank you for supplying my needs, and for your promise to always be with me. That is the secret to contentment.

Sixty-Five

▲▼▲

Law and Order

I understand that somewhere in Texas there's a law on the books that says that criminals must give their victims a twenty-four-hour written or oral notice before they can commit a crime against them. I suppose that's so victims will be sure to have the house clean before it's broken into.

In Tennessee there's a law forbidding you from using a lasso to catch a fish. And in Florida, if you leave an elephant tied too long to a parking meter, you'll have to pay the parking fee just as you would for any other vehicle. I don't know how often they have to enforce these laws, but they are on the books.

South Carolina has a law that requires horses to wear pants at all times. I wonder if there's a provision for shorts in the summer?

New York has a law that makes it a crime to throw a ball at someone's head for fun. That sure takes the joy out of riding the subway, doesn't it?

Laws. At one time these laws probably made a lot of sense, but now they're just outdated and ridiculous, aren't they?

God's laws have always made sense, though. He gave us ten to live our lives by. Jesus shortened them to just two: love God with your whole being, and love your neighbor as yourself. Over the years, well-meaning men and women (or maybe not so well meaning) have tried to add their own laws to God's, and have usually ended up looking silly and irrelevant. Yet

God's original laws have never needed updating. They've held up over time and are just as applicable today as they were when God first gave them to Moses. In fact, many of the laws that govern us today are based upon those original Ten Commandments.

So, follow God's laws. They may not tell you whether you can tie your elephant to a parking meter or if your horse can wear shorts, but they'll help keep you on track in the truly important areas of life.

Thoughts to Ponder

Why do you think God's laws make sense?

Why do you believe some people try to complicate God's laws by adding to them?

Bumper Sticker for the Day

Follow God's ten and win.

Scripture to Stand On

This is the covenant I will make with the house of Israel after that time, declares the Lord. I will put my laws in their minds and write them on their hearts. I will be their God, and they will be my people.

HEBREWS 8:10

Hello Again, Lord ...

Lord, thank you for your Ten Commandments that have never needed updating.

Sixty-Six
▲▼▲

An Obvious Oversight

Not long ago, a body was discovered in a suitcase at an airport. In a news interview, one of the investigating officers said that for the time being it was going to be treated as a suspicious death.

A suspicious death? Did he really think it was going to turn out to be a suicide? "He said he had just one more thing to pack, but how could we have known that he meant himself?"

We all miss the obvious sometimes, don't we? The truth could be right in front of our eyes and we still don't see it.

All of our friends are telling us we've changed. We're more cynical, bitter, and angry than we used to be. But we're blinded to it. We're just having a bad day, we say. Nothing's wrong.

Or maybe we're having a problem with alcohol. Our friends are concerned for us. We tell them to mind their own business. We can control it.

Or maybe it's drugs.

Or stealing.

Or disrespecting our parents.

Or not being thankful.

Or pride and self-centeredness.

Or lack of forgiveness.

Or laziness.

Or sex.

Or gossip.

Or indifference.

Or avoiding the call of God on our lives.

Or any of a hundred other things we might be struggling with. The evidence is there, but we just don't see it. We point to others who are doing the same things we are, or worse. But pointing out their wrongs won't help us any. It only proves we have company, not character.

When a problem becomes so apparent that friends and family are pointing it out to us in love, maybe it's time we take a good hard look at our lives and ask ourselves, "Are we missing the obvious?"

Thoughts to Ponder

Is there an obvious problem in your life that you've been refusing to face?

How do you think God is encouraging you to deal with that problem?

Bumper Sticker for the Day

> Minding your own business is a full-time job.

Scripture to Stand On

For the word of God is living and active. Sharper than any double-edged sword, it penetrates even to dividing soul and spirit, joints and marrow; it judges the thoughts and attitudes of the heart.

HEBREWS 4:12

Hello Again, Lord ...

Lord, help me to see the obvious in my life, and even the not-so-obvious, which only you and I know about. Thank you for helping me as we face these things together.

Sixty-Seven

▲▼▲

For Sale

Have you ever been to a pawnshop? Generally speaking, pawnshops deal with people who need cash fast. They're in some sort of desperate situation, so they look around at their possessions to see what they can pawn for some quick money. Unfortunately, the money offered to them is often far less than the value of the item pawned. After all, the pawnshop owner has to make a living, too.

Yet, believing they don't have any other choice, these desperate individuals go ahead and surrender whatever "prized possession" they brought to pawn. Blinded by their desire or need of the moment, they don't see the value of what they're giving up.

Esau sold his birthright like that. He was desperate and didn't fully realize what he was selling. A birthright isn't something you can easily replace. You won't find one listed on eBay. They don't sell them at Target, or Wal-Mart, or Dillard's. They're one-of-a-kind, and most people hang on to theirs.

But not Esau. Instead of cherishing his birthright and the blessing that came along with it, he, in a sense, pawned it. Esau traded it all in for a bowl of stew. It doesn't even matter if it was the best stew he'd ever eaten, it still wasn't worth the price he paid for it. Yet Esau was desperate, blinded by his desire of the moment.

When Esau finally realized what he'd done (no doubt when he got hungry again and had to face the fact that he'd traded something irreplaceable for something disposable), he felt horrible. That's the way it usually is when we make a bad decision. But it was too late. There were no refunds at Jacob's Diner. The stew was in Esau's belly and Jacob had the birthright. There was no going back.

The moral of the story? Always check the menu prices before ordering your desires. They may end up costing you a lot more than you counted on.

Thoughts to Ponder

Is there something of value that you're on the verge of giving away?

Think about its true worth for a moment. Is it worth more than you're realizing?

Bumper Sticker for the Day

Everything comes with a price, especially our decisions.

Scripture to Stand On

See that no one is sexually immoral, or is godless like Esau, who for a single meal sold his inheritance rights as the oldest son.

HEBREWS 12:16

Hello Again, Lord ...

Lord, help me to cherish those irreplaceable things you've entrusted to me, and, should I ever find myself in a desperate situation, help me to seek sound counsel before acting.

Sixty-Eight

▲▼▲

Do Over

Have you ever been in the middle of leaving a message on someone's answering machine and stumbled over your words or mispronounced your name?

"Hello, Linda, this is Markfuprt ... I mean, Marthansape, I mean, oh, you know who it is. Just call me back."

Or, "Hi, this is Martha. I'm calling to let you know that your filathrupf never arrived and it'll need to be reissionsurated as soon as possible. Thanks."

No matter how badly you'd like to retrieve the message and do it over, you can't. It's on the other person's answering machine and you no longer have control over it.

Sometimes, if we don't think before we talk, we can say things we wish we could retrieve, too. Hurtful things, stupid things, things that make equally little sense. They're out there, taking on a life of their own. But instead of being left on an answering machine, though, they're left on someone's heart, and it's not easy to erase them.

The best solution, then, is to rehearse what we're going to say before we say it. We should send our comments through an editing process in our heads before speaking them. We might even need to do an entire rewrite. After all, the words we say to people could be the last words they hear. We need to make sure they're the ones we want to leave them with.

Thoughts to Ponder

Have you ever said something to someone that you wish you could have taken back?

What do you wish you had done before speaking those words?

Bumper Sticker for the Day

Speaking should go before thinking —
but only in the dictionary.

Scripture to Stand On

Make every effort to live in peace with all men and to be holy; without holiness no one will see the Lord.

HEBREWS 12:14

Hello Again, Lord ...

Lord, when it comes to the words I say to others, help me to be a good editor.

Sixty-Nine

▲▼▲

Run That By Me Again

I love Christmas. I love everything about it—Christmas carols, crowded stores, family gatherings, Christmas pageants, burned cookies, lopsided gingerbread houses, Christmas cards from old and new friends, snow in Tennessee where I now live, suntans in California where I used to live—I love it all. I even shop the day after Christmas for discounted decorations and gifts.

The best part about Christmas is still the Christmas story. It sometimes gets lost in the hustle-bustle, and even though we've all heard it hundreds of times, it is still a remarkable story.

Think about it. A young girl—about the same age as you— was told by God a most incredible thing: She, a virgin, was going to bear his Son. Not only that, but this Son was also going to be the Savior of the world! Wow! There she was, probably right in the middle of doing her math homework, and she was interrupted by God. Now, most of us would love for God to interrupt us in the middle of math homework, wouldn't we? But Mary was interrupted to be told she was going to be the mother of God's only Son! That'd get your mind off long division pretty fast, wouldn't it?

Hebrews deals a lot with faith, but imagine the faith Mary had, to handle what she was going to be faced with in the months to come. She was going to have to tell her family and all of her friends that she was pregnant by the power of the Holy Ghost.

Put yourself in Mary's shoes. Or even Joseph's. Do you think you would have had the faith to handle a situation like this? Would you have doubted what you heard God say to you? Or, if you were Joseph, would you have doubted Mary's faithfulness? If you were one of Mary's friends, how do you think you would have reacted to the news of her pregnancy? Would you have believed her, or would she have become a topic of discussion for your lunch table at school?

It took a lot of faith for Mary and Joseph to do what God had asked them to do. It takes a lot of faith for us to do what God wants us to do, too. And sometimes it even takes a lot of faith just to be a friend.

Thoughts to Ponder

How do you think Mary's friends might have reacted when they found out about her news?

What kind of a friend do you think you would have been to Mary? To Joseph?

Bumper Sticker for the Day

Friends should never be a disappearing act.

Scripture to Stand On

And again, when God brings his firstborn into the world, he says, "Let all God's angels worship him."

HEBREWS 1:6

Hello Again, Lord ...

Lord, help all my friendships to be faithful ones.

Seventy

▲▼▲

Busted

Getting grounded isn't much fun, is it? Neither is having your allowance taken away, serving a time out, getting detention, writing "I will not ride the ceiling fan" five hundred times on a chalkboard, or receiving a swat on the backside. Nobody likes to be punished for something they did wrong. But without punishment of some kind, we'd probably never learn any of life's important lessons.

If our mothers or fathers didn't punish us for running into the middle of the street during rush-hour traffic, we'd no doubt keep doing it until an ambulance takes us away. If we didn't have to serve detention for fighting at school, we'd never learn that fighting isn't the way to handle disagreements. If we weren't punished for putting stink bombs in the girls' cabin at camp, who knows what we'd try to do next? Discipline helps us to know which behavior is acceptable and which is not. It lets us know there are consequences for our actions. It gives us boundaries ahead of time, so that those boundaries are not imposed upon us by force in a worse situation.

When I was young, not only did I hate getting into trouble, I also hated to see other people get into trouble. Yet I knew that discipline was necessary for our own protection. When we did something we shouldn't have, we needed to be punished in order to make sure we got the message.

Do you know that, just like the other authority figures in your life, God also wants to keep you from trouble? He knows if he were to let you make up your own rules as you went along, you'd no doubt end up with some real problems. So he disciplines you much like a loving parent would discipline his or her child. He wants you to get the message.

So the next time you don't get what you want when you want it, you might want to consider the possibility that you're in one of God's "time outs." Maybe you need to sit still a while and think about that wrong decision you made, or that ungodly behavior you exhibited. Maybe you're serving a little holy detention. Is this because God wants to punish you and deprive you of your wants? No. It's because he loves you and wants to do what's best for you in the long run.

Thoughts to Ponder

Have you ever felt like you were in one of God's "time outs"?

Why do you think God chooses to sometimes show us his love in discipline?

Bumper Sticker for the Day

> God—the ultimate "Father of the Year"

Scripture to Stand On

Our fathers disciplined us for a little while as they thought best; but God disciplines us for our good, that we may share in his holiness. No discipline seems pleasant at the time, but painful. Later on, however, it produces a harvest of righteousness and peace for those who have been trained by it.

HEBREWS 12:10,11

Hello Again, Lord ...

Lord, thank you for your discipline. Sometimes it hurts, but it always works.

Seventy-One

▲▼▲

Best Laid Plans

There's an old saying, "The best-laid plans of mice and men often go astray." This means that no matter how much you've planned for something, no matter what precautions you've taken for all the things that could go wrong, something unexpected still could go awry.

Just because we've gotten our parent's permission to go to that party on Friday night, just because we've bought a new outfit, just because we've arranged transportation and saved enough money for our ticket, doesn't mean we're going to be at that party.

Life is full of unpredictability. The weather could turn threatening, we could have an unexpected family emergency, or we could win two million dollars in the Reader's Digest sweepstakes and decide to celebrate at Arby's—in short, anything could happen.

When I was growing up, my parents would always follow any announcement of plans with "... the good Lord willing."

"We're going on vacation to Arkansas this summer ... the good Lord willing."

"Yes, you can go to the sleepover this weekend ... the good Lord willing."

"OK, you can take your homemade brownies to your classroom ... the good Lord willing."

They understood that God is the one who is ultimately in control, and they saw the wisdom in leaving that control to him. (They also wanted to have an out because my brownies were known to throw out the suspension in our Buick.)

So, the next time you're making plans, remember to leave the last word with God. Hebrews tells us to say "And God permitting, we will do so" whenever we make plans. If we have that "good Lord willing" attitude, then when our plans are changed without notice we'll be able to rest assured that what's best for our lives will indeed transpire—not according to our plans, but to his.

Thoughts to Ponder

Do you get frustrated when plans that you've made fall through?

Can you think of a time when you were glad that your plans fell through, because God's plans were better?

Bumper Sticker for the Day

> The best-laid plans are laid in God's hands.

Scripture to Stand On

And God permitting, we will do so.

HEBREWS 6:3

Hello Again, Lord ...

Lord, may I always give you the ultimate control of my plans.

Seventy-Two

▲▼▲

Heart of Stone

There are several scriptures in the book of Hebrews that warn us against hardening our hearts. This isn't a biblical plea to get our cholesterol checked. (Though the Scripture about honoring our bodies as the temple of the Holy Spirit probably covers that, as well as skydiving without a parachute, and eating my cooking. But I digress.)

In Hebrews Paul is warning us about hardening our hearts toward God.

Hardening one's heart is often a protective act. If we've been hurt by someone and we don't want to keep getting hurt, we put up a shield. The shield, we figure, will protect us. Yet that same shield can keep true friends out, too. That's what Paul is warning us against. He knows life is full of hurts—people who are going to let us down, say or do cruel things, and basically prove to be anything but friends. He also knows that it's our human nature to protect ourselves, to harden our hearts toward hurtful people, and to hide behind our shield of protection. What he wants us to avoid is hardening our hearts toward God. It's not God who has let us down. It's not God who has hurt us. It's not God who has been less than a friend.

God wants us to keep an open heart toward him, one that's sensitive to his leading. A hardened heart can protect us from the hurts of this world in the short term, but in the long run, it will always do us more harm than good. It can keep love out as well as pain. And it could eventually keep God out, too.

Thoughts to Ponder

Have you ever been in a situation where you felt you had to harden your heart to protect yourself?

Why do you think God wants us to keep an open heart toward him?

Bumper Sticker for the Day

A heart of stone isn't a monument.

Scripture to Stand On

Therefore God again set a certain day, calling it Today, when a long time later he spoke through David, as was said before: "Today, if you hear his voice, do not harden your hearts."

HEBREWS 4:7

Hello Again, Lord ...

Lord, help me to remember that a hardened heart may not hurt, but it doesn't feel, either.

Seventy-Three

▲▼▲

I Believe in You

I believe in you.

I believe there's a purpose for your life. You were no accident.

I believe in your dreams. They're not impossible.

I believe you're better than your mistakes. They don't define you—never have, never will.

I believe every day is a new opportunity for you, and I can't wait to see what you'll do with it.

I believe that no matter what you face in life, you can survive and it will ultimately benefit you.

I believe you already have what you need to make the right choices, but I'll still love you even when you don't.

I believe in you when you feel like giving up.

I believe in your talents and abilities, and am convinced you're the perfect one for the work I have in mind.

I believe in you even if I'm the only one who does. And I'm enough.

I believe in the person you can become, but I accept you right now as you are.

I believe you're valuable.

I believe you're unique and irreplaceable.

I believe you're worth dying for.

I believe in you.

…Jesus

Thoughts to Ponder

Why do you think Jesus believes in you?

When someone believes in you this much, how do you think you should respond?

Bumper Sticker for the Day

> Behind every good success story is a God who believed it could happen.

Scripture to Stand On

You made him a little lower than the angels; you crowned him with glory and honor.

HEBREWS 2:7

Hello Again, Lord ...

Lord, when it comes to appraising our worth, thank you for seeing it even when we don't.

Seventy-Four
▲▼▲

Perfectly Time Trouble

One night my car died in the middle of the road for no apparent reason. There I was, in the fast lane of a main street with a car that wasn't moving. Several times I tried to flag down passing drivers to ask for help in pushing my car to the side of the road, but they all just pulled around me and went on their way, giving me a few aggravated honks as they went. Not one person wanted to get involved. I realize that in this day and age you need to be careful, but we were at a busy intersection. Hundreds of other people were around. Someone could have offered to call a tow truck or the police for me. Yet no one did.

The main reason why no one offered to help me, I think, was due to the fact that my problem had presented itself at an inopportune time. It was around five o'clock, and people were rushing home from work. They didn't want to be bothered with someone else's problems. Had my car been more considerate and stalled out on a Saturday afternoon, they would have been more inclined to help. Or had it been blocking traffic on their way to work instead of on their way home, they might have stopped. After all, helping a stranded motorist is a great excuse for missing that first hour of work. But my problem was going to inconvenience them, not get them out of something. So they drove on by.

When those around us have spiritual or life problems, their pleas for help don't always come at opportune times for us, either. Often they present themselves without any warning whatsoever. We might be moving along just fine when all of a sudden someone stalls out in front of us. Just like the drivers on the road that night, we can either stop and offer help, or drive on by. The choice is ours.

Thoughts to Ponder

Have you ever ignored someone else's problem because it presented itself at an inopportune time?

How does it make you feel when you need help and no one offers it to you?

Bumper Sticker for the Day

> **Trouble never makes reservations.**

Scripture to Stand On

Remember those in prison as if you were their fellow prisoners, and those who are mistreated as if you yourselves were suffering.

HEBREWS 13:3

Hello Again, Lord ...

Lord, help me to be as ready to help others when they're hurting as I'd like them to be ready to help me.

Seventy-Five
▲▼▲

By Any Other Name

There is a town in Illinois called "Normal." There's one in both Arkansas and North Dakota called "Hope." There's a city in Alabama called "Love," and one in South Dakota called "Faith." There's a Plain, Wisconsin, and a Crook County in Oregon. The name of a city or town doesn't necessarily describe its inhabitants, does it? Just because someone lives in Hope doesn't mean that person has hope in his or her life, and moving to Love isn't necessarily going to bring more love your way. I'm also pretty sure there are faithless people living in Faith, as well as many wonderful, law-abiding citizens living in Crook County.

The people who live in Mount Pleasant, South Carolina, may very well be pleasant, but as far as I know they don't have to be to live there. Furthermore, I'm reasonably sure you don't have to be a twin with an equilibrium problem to live in Twin Falls, Idaho, or be on a bowling team to live in Bowling Green, Kentucky. I also doubt that you have to be a rock to live in Round Rock, Texas. (If you do, I'm sure my biscuits would qualify.)

The point is that it doesn't matter what is written on the sign at the entrance to a city. They're only words, and words won't tell you a thing about the people living there.

Some of us think that if we wear the label of Christian it'll make us one. We assume the title is enough. Yet being a Christian isn't about a title, or how many rules we can follow, or how many good deeds we can do. It's about accepting a free gift of grace and sharing that same gift just as freely with others. We can go to church every Sunday, recite all the Christian lingo, and still not truly believe, in our hearts. Yet that's the part of us that God looks at to determine our faith in him: Not our words, not our deeds, but our hearts.

Thoughts to Ponder

Why do you think God is more interested in our hearts than in labels?

Where do you think your heart stands with God?

Bumper Sticker for the Day

Witness wear means little without the witness.

Scripture to Stand On

For this reason Christ is the mediator of a new covenant, that those who are called may receive the promised eternal inheritance—now that he has died as a ransom to set them free from the sins committed under the first covenant.

HEBREWS 9:15

Hello Again, Lord ...

Thank you, Lord, for your grace that can't be bought, can't be earned, and can't be hidden from others.

Seventy-Six

Is there someone in your life who intimidates you? It could be a classmate, a sibling, or someone you don't even know but have to walk by every day on your way to class. Whoever it is that's trying to make you feel inferior, that person no doubt feels inferior him- or herself.

Yet, knowing why some people intimidate others doesn't make their actions any easier to tolerate, does it? Over the years I've had to deal with bullies who've easily intimidated me. I have a "peace at any cost" personality, so it takes an awful lot before I'll finally stand up for myself. The older I get, though, the more I realize that there are times when we need to hold our ground. The years we waste being a doormat (which isn't what God called us to be) would be better spent following our true calling.

Jesus was meek, but I don't think anyone would classify him as weak. Jesus was a man of peace, but I've never heard him described as a pushover. There is a difference, then, between willfully seeking peace from a position of strength and being intimidated into peace from a position of fear.

God covers the subject of bullies in Hebrews. He tells us that we don't have to be afraid of them. Our hope, our trust, is in him; therefore, we needn't fear what anyone else can do to us.

Bullies appear throughout the Scriptures. They showed up in families. Joseph's brothers were bullies. Bullies showed up on the battlefield. Goliath was a bully. They even were in politics. Herod was a bully. Bullies showed up on the religious scene. The Pharisees could be classified as bullies because they kept trying to make Jesus look foolish in front of the people. In each instance, though, the faithful stood strong on their faith and it was the bully who was eventually humbled.

In Hebrews, we learn that we don't have to allow someone to intimidate us into doing something we shouldn't do, or into not doing something we should do. He reminds us that God is our helper, and we needn't live in fear of anyone. Not even a bully.

Thoughts to Ponder

Do you have a bully in your life?

If so, are you allowing him or her to keep you from living your life to its fullest potential?

Bumper Sticker for the Day

> No one would bully you if they could
> see who you have backing you up.

Scripture to Stand On

So we say with confidence, "The Lord is my helper; I will not be afraid. What can man do to me?"

HEBREWS 13:6

Hello Again, Lord ...

Lord, forgive me when I've forgotten who I've got on my side.

Seventy-Seven
▲▼▲

Planting Time

I didn't really enjoy horticulture class. It wasn't much fun watching everyone else's seeds sprout and bloom while mine just lay there beneath the dirt and took a semester-long nap. I couldn't even get weeds to grow. Not in the ground anyway. But now in my locker? That was a cinch.

I did learn one thing in horticulture class, though. I learned that the condition of the soil is very important. If it's too sandy or too rocky, or if you don't water it enough, you're probably not going to have a very good crop.

Paul tells us in Hebrews that we should think about what kind of soil we are. (See, there's a reason to keep some of that dirt behind our ears.) God wants us to be productive, fertile land—in other words, land he can work with. He wants the very best to come from us, not just weeds or undernourished foliage.

So how do we become fertile land? By not allowing the rocky places in life to leave crushing boulders in our attitude. By letting the tumbleweeds of old grudges and lack of forgiveness roll on their way. By refusing to get buried under the sands of discouragement that happen to blow by. And by allowing the rain of the Holy Spirit to daily refresh us.

Fertile soil is what is needed to have a productive garden. It's what's needed for a productive life, too.

Thoughts to Ponder

What kind of land do you think you are right now?

If you don't feel you're as fertile as God would like you to be, what steps are you willing to take today to become the kind of land that God can work with?

Bumper Sticker for the Day

> Your life—garden or toxic waste dump?
> It all depends on what you allow into it.

Scripture to Stand On

But land that produces thorns and thistles is worthless and is in danger of being cursed. In the end it will be burned.

HEBREWS 6:8

Hello Again, Lord ...

Lord, thank you for being a caring gardener, wanting only the very best to grow in my life.

Seventy-Eight

▲▼▲

A Not-So-Perfect Landing

On Sunday, March 5, 2000, a Boeing 737 with 142 people on board skidded off a rain-slick runway at Burbank Airport, smashing through a fence and hitting a car before coming to a stop at a nearby Chevron gas station. Luckily, no one was seriously injured, but I'm sure it cost the gas station some business. After all, who wants to wait in line behind an airplane at a gas station?

The reason I mention this incident is because one of the people on board that aircraft was an employee of the company where my husband happened to be working as Security Manager, and, believe it or not, she faithfully reported to work that next morning.

Now, if anyone had an excuse for staying home, this woman did. She had just survived a terrifying experience. It's not every day that your plane not only takes you to your gate, but gives you a tour of beautiful downtown Burbank, too. I can't imagine what it must have been like for those passengers. Not only did their lives flash in front of their eyes; so did billboards, streetlights, and telephone poles.

Yet, at least one of those passengers was dedicated enough to report for work the next day. It kind of makes that scratchy throat that keeps you home from school pale by comparison, doesn't it?

Dependability is one of the qualities that employers, teachers, and civic leaders look for in an individual. It doesn't matter how many noble acts you say you're going to do if you never get around to doing them. It doesn't matter if you say you'll help with the party on Friday night if you don't show up to help. It doesn't matter if you raise your hand and pledge to send money to a missionary if it never ends up in the envelope.

That lady had made a commitment to be at work the next day, and she showed up. She had a perfectly acceptable excuse for staying home for a few days, but she chose not to. She was dedicated, and I'm sure that dedication was noted. Dedicated people are people you can count on, rain or shine, good landings or bad.

Thoughts to Ponder

When you promise something, do you follow through, or do you look for excuses for why you couldn't get around to it?

Why do you think it's important to be a person who can be counted on?

Bumper Sticker for the Day

Commitment that can't be counted on doesn't count.

Scripture to Stand On

But Christ is faithful as a son over God's house. And we are his house, if we hold on to our courage and the hope of which we boast.
HEBREWS 3:6

Hello Again, Lord ...

Lord, help me to follow through on my promises to you, just as you always follow through on your promises to me.

Seventy-Nine

▲▼▲

Don't Push It

God is love. But he's also just. Disappointed with man's disobedience, he once destroyed every living thing on earth except Noah and those who were with him on the ark. He's taken kingdoms away from prideful kings and given them to shepherd boys. He destroyed Sodom and Gomorrah with fire from heaven. Adam and Eve disobeyed him and were evicted from the Garden of Eden. Lot's wife disobeyed and became a pillar of salt. Moses disobeyed and was not allowed to see the Promised Land. God's forgiving, but holy. Patient, but firm. Loving, but just.

In Hebrews 10, verses 28 and 29, Paul reminds us that "anyone who rejected the law of Moses died without mercy," and he goes on to say, "how much more severely do you think a man deserves to be punished who has trampled the Son of God under foot, who has treated as an unholy thing the blood of the covenant that sanctified him, and who has insulted the Spirit of grace?"

God is everything the Bible says he is: loving, patient, full of grace and mercy, one who can be trusted, one who'll never leave us or forsake us, our healer, our provider, our Abba father. Yet the Bible also tells us that God cannot look upon sin. He has given us laws, and they're to be kept.

God tells us he is a jealous God. He doesn't want us putting anything before him. That's understandable. If you had sacrificed your only son for someone, I'm sure you'd feel the same way. God wants 100 percent of our commitment. He wants 100 percent of our love. He wants 100 percent of us. Not a bad price to pay for 100 percent of his grace.

Thoughts to Ponder

Why do you think God wants us to obey his laws?

Why do you think God is a jealous God?

Bumper Sticker for the Day

A just God just wants obedience.

Scripture to Stand On

It is a dreadful thing to fall into the hands of the living God.
HEBREWS 10:31

Hello Again, Lord ...

Lord, help me to honor your gift of grace by obeying your laws.

Eighty

▲▼▲

Say "Ahh"

Don't you love going to the dentist?

What kind of a question is that, right? Of course, you don't love it. You may not hate it. You may be able to tolerate it better than most other people. But chances are, you don't *love* it.

Believe it or not, visiting the dentist used to be an even worse ordeal. In the days before Novocain was widely used, dentists would work on teeth without any anesthetic whatsoever. Patients would have to sit there with their mouths gaping open while the dentist drilled to his or her heart's content. It was especially fun when they'd hit a nerve and the patient's fingernails would pierce through the armrest (or the dentist's arm, whichever was easier to reach).

With Novocain and other numbing drugs, the dentist is no longer our enemy. By deadening the feeling in our gums, we're able to tolerate the pain and discomfort of dental work a lot more easily. We still don't enjoy it, but for the most part we can tolerate it. Numbness does that. It keeps us from feeling what we normally would feel.

As a society, we've become numb to more than just drilling and filling. We've become numb to changes in morality, too. Nothing shocks us anymore. Things that used to bring us discomfort, no longer do. We tolerate more, we accept more, we overlook more. Our boundaries have been crossed so many times, we don't know where the lines are or even remember where they used to be.

That's unfortunate. Why? Because not only does God want us to love righteousness and hate iniquity, he also promises us an anointing of joy if we do. So the next time you find yourself feeling uncomfortable about a certain situation, remember that discomfort just might be there for your own, and society's, good.

Now as for those root canals? Bring on the Novocain!

Thoughts to Ponder

Do you feel your "discomfort level" is as keen today as it was last year?

Why do you think God doesn't want you to numb your internal shock detectors?

Bumper Sticker for the Day

What you accept today is hard to fight against tomorrow.

Scripture to Stand On

Thou hast loved righteousness and hated iniquity; therefore God, even thy God, hath anointed thee with the oil of gladness above thy fellows.

HEBREWS 1:9, KJV

Hello Again, Lord ...

Lord, give me the courage to defend my convictions before they need life support.

Eighty-One

▲▼▲

Out of Nothing

Don't you hate it when you get ready to cook something and find that you don't have one of the ingredients? I once made a meatloaf using sweetened cereal as the filler because I didn't have any breadcrumbs. Meatloaf wasn't meant to be made with sweetened cereal. It's like putting whipped cream on a pot roast or butterscotch syrup on spaghetti. It wasn't very good. The cat wouldn't even eat it. Obviously, she wants to hang onto all of her nine lives.

My son has learned to improvise in the kitchen, too. He once served us some homemade soup that he had cooked. We didn't have any beef or chicken in the house, so I wasn't sure what he had used for meat, but we all sampled it anyway. It was good, but it had an unusual flavor. When we asked what kind of soup it was, he proudly announced, "Tuna Soup."

Cooking without one of the major ingredients of a recipe will usually produce less than desirable results. Yet imagine if you had to make something out of absolutely nothing. Not a single ingredient was there. That's how God created the world. Out of nothing. He spoke and it was there. All of it. The earth, the heavens, the animals, the creatures of the sea, and man. They all came from nothing. It wasn't as if he was making the rhinoceros and discovered he had nothing to make the horn out of, or was in the middle of creating man and discovered he had somehow forgotten the lips. He made everything by simply speaking it into existence. Man, the world, the entire universe ... all out of nothing. Pretty incredible, huh? Kind of makes the tuna soup pale by comparison, doesn't it?

Thoughts to Ponder

Have you ever had to improvise on a recipe or project?

What one word would you use to describe the creativity and power of God?

Bumper Sticker for Today

> When God speaks, things happen.

Scripture to Stand On

By faith we understand that the universe was formed at God's command, so that what is seen was not made out of what was visible.

HEBREWS 11:3

Hello Again, Lord ...

Lord, when I think of all you've created, surely I can trust you with my life.

Eighty-Two

▲▼▲

How's the Weather

Just as there are fair-weather friends (friends who stand by you only in the good times), there are foul-weather friends, too (friends who come around only when things aren't going that well ... for them).

Foul-weather friends are your closest buddies when they need you. If they need a ride to the mall, your phone rings. If they're failing science class, you get asked to "help" them with their homework. If they don't know anyone else at that St. Patrick's Day party, they'll spend the entire evening chatting with you by the six-foot-long submarine sandwich. If their parents won't let them practice the tuba at home anymore, they'll come over to your house and practice all weekend.

They're your best friends ... when it's advantageous for them to be. Yet the minute their social lives, grades, or tuba skills take an upswing, they disappear faster than tickets to the Super Bowl. They're foul-weather friends, and their friendship is as unpredictable as a tornado.

You may not be able to do much about foul-weather friendships, other than see them for what they are, but you can keep yourself from becoming one yourself. Ann Landers once said, "The measure of a man is how he treats someone who can do him absolutely no good." When it comes to your friends, are you there for them at all times, or just when you need them? Do you have one set of friends who are steadfast and faithful, who you can always count on to be there when you're feeling low, and another group you hang around with when your life is going great?

Be a friend who's a friend in all seasons, and surround yourself with the same kind of people.

Thoughts to Ponder

Why do you think foul weather friends are friends you can't count on?

Would you say you've been a true friend or a foul-weather friend? How can you start being a true friend to those you love?

Bumper Sticker for the Day

Friendship—it's not a seasonal thing.

Scripture to Stand On

Keep on loving each other as brothers.

HEBREWS 13:1

Hello Again, Lord ...

Lord, thank you for being a friend at all times. Help me to be that kind of friend to others.

Eighty-Three

▲▼▲

The Price

Moses had everything. Or so it seemed. As an infant, he had been taken in by Pharaoh's daughter and raised as her own child in the lap of luxury. Moses was educated by the finest scholars of the day, wore the most expensive clothes, had the fastest chariots at his disposal, and was beloved by Pharaoh. The kid had it made.

There was something inside Moses, however, that told him he had a higher calling. He couldn't explain it, but he knew his life was about more than just being a member of Pharaoh's household. God had a plan for Moses' life. He had spared him as an infant for a distinct purpose, and even though on the outside it seemed like Moses had already attained more notoriety and riches than the average person would ever attain in his or her lifetime, God had so much more in store for Moses.

Yet Moses had to give up a few things in order to follow the will of God for his life. He had to leave the comfort zone of Pharaoh's palace and associate himself with the Hebrew slaves. He had to risk rejection from those same Hebrews, once he let them know of his true heritage and mission. "Moses is going to lead us out of bondage? But he's one of them!" I'm sure they grumbled as this "outsider" tried to organize their exodus. And even after he led them out of Egypt, he had to listen to them grumble and complain that they "never should have left Egypt. Moses just brought us out here to die!" Following God's plan for his life wasn't an easy journey for Moses.

It's not always easy for us, either.

God's will always comes at a price. It's not the same price for everyone, but there is always a price. Moses was willing to pay it, and the children of Israel (those who didn't doubt) at long last did get to see the Promised Land. There's a promised land in your life, too. Are you willing to make the commitment and sacrifice to reach it?

Thoughts to Ponder

Why do you think there is a price to fulfilling God's will in your life?

Why do you think following God's will for your life is always worth the price?

Bumper Sticker for the Day

The price of God's will always proves to be a bargain.

Scripture to Stand On

By faith Moses, when he had grown up, refused to be known as the son of Pharaoh's daughter. He chose to be mistreated along with the people of God rather than to enjoy the pleasures of sin for a short time.

HEBREWS 11:24-25

Hello Again, Lord ...

Lord, help me to be willing to pay the price to fulfill your plans for my life.

Eighty-Four

▲▼▲

Failed Again

What if, after having received all A's and B's in English class throughout the entire semester, you get a D on one test and your teacher decides to give you a D for the class? That wouldn't seem fair, would it? That one D doesn't reflect the kind of student you are. You slipped up on one test, not the whole school year. You're a good student who just had a bad day. Maybe you didn't study like you should have studied. Or maybe you did study, but were in a post-lunch coma and couldn't stay awake long enough to answer all the questions. Whatever went wrong, it was temporary. It's not a true reflection of your yearlong effort.

Or what if you did slip up for an entire school year? Your GPA ended up being 0.2, but before that you were a good student, maybe even on the honor roll. Yet this one particular year, you got sidetracked and failed. Does that mean you're a failure?

Absolutely not!

Someone once said that failure is an act, not a person. Just because you mess up on one test, or one year, or two years, that doesn't mean that you become your failure. We all mess up. Sometimes it's a small failure and we get back on track quickly; other times it's a big one and it takes us a little longer. Yet even if our friends have abandoned us, even if our parents have lost faith in us, even if we don't believe in ourselves anymore, God hasn't given up on us. We mean more to him than our mistakes. If we didn't, why would he be willing to sacrifice his own son in our place? He didn't do it because we were doing everything right. He looked down at us in the middle of our failures and still saw hope.

If you don't learn anything else in life, learn this: you mean an awful lot to God. He's not going to give up on you because you fail one test. Or two. Or a dozen. Naturally, he wants you to get high marks in life, to achieve, to become everything that's in his plan for you to become. But he loves you beyond your works. He loves you in spite of your failures. He loves you not because of who you are or aren't, but because of who he is.

Thoughts to Ponder

How does it feel to know that God still loves you in the middle of your failures?

Why can't we "earn" God's love?

Bumper Sticker for the Day

The dress code in heaven? Grace.

Scripture to Stand On

How much more, then, will the blood of Christ, who through the eternal Spirit offered himself unblemished to God, cleanse our consciences from acts that lead to death, so that we may serve the living God!

HEBREWS 9:14

Hello Again, Lord ...

Lord, thank you for reminding me that it is your love, not my failures, that defines who I am.

Eighty-Five

▲▼▲

An Inside Job

The Bible is full of accounts of people who learned important lessons from being on the "inside."

Adam and Eve were inside the Garden of Eden when they learned just how important obedience is to God. (They also learned that a new outfit isn't always the answer to your problems.)

Noah was inside the ark when he discovered that God is a fulfiller of his promises. (No doubt he also learned that it's not a good idea to put two elephants on the same side of a boat as two rhinoceroses.)

Jonah was inside a big fish when he learned it's always better to follow God's calling than to run from it ... unless, of course, you enjoy sleeping with your sushi.

The people of Jericho were inside their man-made walls when they learned that man's best masonry is still no match for God.

Lazarus was inside the tomb when he found out that his friend Jesus had authority over death and the grave.

Paul and Silas were inside a jail cell when they learned that guards, chains, and locks couldn't separate them from the love of God.

And Jesus was inside a manger inside a stable when the world learned that God had just given the world his ultimate gift of love.

Faith? It's usually an "inside" job, too.

Thoughts to Ponder

Do you feel your relationship with God is a personal one?

Why do you think God wants us to have a personal relationship with him?

Bumper Sticker for the Day

When it comes to your life, God wants to be an insider.

Scripture to Stand On

And without faith it is impossible to please God, because anyone who comes to him must believe that he exists and that he rewards those who earnestly seek him.

HEBREWS 11:6

Hello Again, Lord ...

Lord, may you always feel welcome inside my life.

Eighty-Six

▲▼▲

Simply Speaking

"Ticket," the usher said as the young man approached the door to the auditorium.

"Here," the young man answered.

Reading off the ticket, the usher said, "Row G, Seat 46," then pointed him in the direction he should go.

"How much more do I owe?" the young man asked.

"Nothing. You've got your ticket, so just go on in and take your seat."

"Do you take credit cards?"

"No, but you already have your ticket anyway."

"Can I write you a check?"

"No need to," the usher assured him, shrugging his shoulders apologetically at the long line of people that had now formed behind him. "You've got your ticket. Go on in."

"I might have a half-price coupon," the young man said, quickly searching through his wallet.

"But you already have your ticket."

"Well, if you won't take cash, credit cards, my personal check, or a discount coupon, how am I supposed to get in?"

"You have a ticket in your hand, so you've obviously RSVP'd. That's all there is to it."

"I get it now. You want me to use a debit card."

"Look, you're not getting the picture here. You have the ticket in your hand. You've done what you needed to do to get in, and that was RSVP. You accepted the invitation, and now we accept your admittance."

The young man threw his ticket down to the ground and walked away in a huff.

"Hey, where are you going?" the usher called out after him.

"Nobody told me it was a private party."

Obviously, this scene never really took place. Yet that's how some of us treat the gospel message. We can't comprehend that it's as simple as it is. We think there has to be more to it than God loving us so much that he gave his Son to die in our place, and if we believe in him, we will have eternal life. We figure there has to be some other requirement for us to receive this gift. Yet other than turning in our RSVP, there isn't. The gospel message is simple. We should quit making it so hard.

Thoughts to Ponder

Why do you think God made his gospel plan simple?

In what ways do you think we have been making the gospel message more difficult than it should be?

Bumper Sticker for the Day

To put it simply, God put it simply.

Scripture to Stand On

So Christ was sacrificed once to take away the sins of many people; and he will appear a second time, not to bear sin, but to bring salvation to those who are waiting for him.

HEBREWS 9:28

Hello Again, Lord ...

Thank you, Lord, for the simplicity of the gospel.

Eighty-Seven

▲▼▲

Walk a Mile in My Pain

Ever wonder why you've had to deal with certain temptations? Or why you've had to overcome extreme obstacles,
or been repeatedly forced to come face to face with your
doubts?

It could be so that you'll be able to help others.

Think about it. If you were having health problems, would
it help to have a bodybuilder who's in the best of shape tell you
that you need to trust God for your health and healing? If you
were having financial problems, would it help to know that Bill
Gates feels for you? What about temptations? Does it encourage you to hear from those who smugly say they've never been
tempted in the area where you're tempted? Or does it help to
hear from someone who's been there, too?

When we go through things ourselves, it makes us sensitive
to others who are going through the same thing. Or at least it
should. That could be why God allows us to go through trying
situations. It validates our own faith to us, and it gives us a message of hope for others. After all, if you can trust God for that
health problem, others know they can, too. If you can have
faith in the midst of disappointments, so can your friends. And
if you can resist temptation in a certain area, then other people will know they can resist it as well.

So the next time you think about that test you're facing,
remember you don't just need to pass it for yourself, but for
everyone who's watching you, too.

Thoughts to Ponder

Can you think of something in your life that could be an encouragement to others?

Think of something difficult that you or one of your friends is going through right now. Who do you know that has faced a similar circumstance that could be an encouragement?

Bumper Sticker for the Day

The best testimony comes from another patient.

Scripture to Stand On

He is able to deal gently with those who are ignorant and are going astray, since he himself is subject to weakness.

HEBREWS 5:2

Hello Again, Lord ...

Lord, help me to remember that how I handle my difficulties could help someone else handle theirs.

Eighty-Eight

▲▼▲

Respectfully Speaking

One of the songs Aretha Franklin is best known for is the classic "R-E-S-P-E-C-T." It's a song that talks about not getting the respect she deserves.

Maybe God should have dedicated an entire book in the Bible to this subject as it relates to him. Since the creation of man, God hasn't been getting the respect he deserves, either.

Adam and Eve didn't show God much respect when they decided to disobey him. Their son Cain didn't show him respect when he allowed jealousy and sin to enter into his life, leading him to commit the very first murder-one in history. Goliath didn't show God respect when he taunted the army of Israel. Jonah didn't show him respect either when he decided to try running away from his calling.

And so the disrespect has continued through the years, and still exists today. When we place others or our own desires before God, we're not showing him respect. When we don't listen when he's speaking to us through his Word, we're not showing him respect. When we don't appreciate the blessings he's giving us, we're not showing him respect. When we let him down, we're not showing him respect. When we use his name in vain, we're not showing him respect. When we take him for granted, we're not showing him respect. When we let others disrespect him, we're not showing him respect. When we make him wait, we're not showing him respect. When we fail to follow through on what he wants us to do, we're not showing him respect. When we're too tired to talk to him, we're not showing him respect. R-E-S-P-E-C-T. Maybe it's time we all showed God a little more of it.

Thoughts to Ponder

Do you feel you give God the respect he deserves?

Why do you think it's important to show God respect at all times?

Bumper Sticker for the Day

An awesome God should never be treated
like an afterthought.

Scripture to Stand On

Therefore, since we are receiving a kingdom that cannot be shaken, let us be thankful, and so worship God acceptably with reverence and awe.

HEBREWS 12:28

Hello Again, Lord ...

Lord, forgive me for the times when I've shown others or myself more respect than I've shown you.

Eighty-Nine
▲▼▲

Stressed? Who Me?

Maybe it's just me, but I've been noticing an awful lot of stress-related products on the market recently. Tabletop waterfalls, back massagers, bath spas, nature sounds CD's, aroma candles—on and on it goes. Walk through any mall or department store in our great nation and one would get the distinct impression that Americans are under a good amount of stress.

We are. In fact, a lot of us are off the chart. There are, no doubt, a number of reasons for this. One is the fact that everything has been speeded up. We used to write letters, mail them, then wait a few weeks for a response. Now we write E-mail and it's instantaneous. We used to have down time, we'd get away from the phone and go for walks or sit by a brook and just relax. Now, if we do that, we've got a beeper, a cell phone, and an alarm watch going off simultaneously. We also used to live in smaller communities, where our friendships had to survive. Now, relationships are more disposable. If this friend doesn't work out, we erase his or her number off our direct dial and move on to someone else. Lifelong friendships are stress-busting, comforting in the midst of life's madness, yet all too often we shortsightedly throw them away.

Another source of our stress is in the fact that we've become more self-dependent and less God-dependent. This is not a smart move. Self has its limitations. God doesn't.

Hebrews talks a lot about "resting in the Lord." God didn't

intend for us to be under this much stress. He knows it's not good for us. And since he created the universe and is a God who loves and cares for us more than anything else, living in fear and worry is simply not necessary.

Thoughts to Ponder

Do you feel you've been under too much stress lately?

Why do you think God wants you to enter into his rest?

Bumper Sticker for the Day

Rest ye in the Lord ... but not in English class.

Scripture to Stand On

Now we who have believed enter that rest.

HEBREWS 4:3

Hello Again, Lord ...

Lord, when I'm feeling stressed, help me to remember my rest is in you.

Ninety
▲▼▲

Amazing Plans

God has an amazing plan for your life ... even when you're clueless.

God has an amazing plan for your life ... even when you're scared.

God has an amazing plan for your life ... even when you think you're not qualified.

God has an amazing plan for your life ... even when you think you don't deserve it.

God has an amazing plan for your life ... even when you've already wasted a lot of time.

God has an amazing plan for your life ... even when you wish he'd use someone else.

God has an amazing plan for your life ... even when it seems unattainable.

God has an amazing plan for your life ... even if your plans are already in motion.

God has an amazing plan for your life ... even when you're feeling your lowest.

God has an amazing plan for your life ... even when others don't see it.

God has an amazing plan for your life ... even when you're willing to settle for less.

God has an amazing plan for your life ... even after you've let him down. Again. And again. And again.

God has an amazing plan for your life!

Thoughts to Ponder

Knowing that God has an amazing plan for your life, what do you think you should be doing about it?

Why do you think God would invest so much of his love and time in you?

Bumper Sticker for the Day

Got plans for your life? God has better ones.

Scripture to Stand On

But there is a place where someone has testified: "What is man that you are mindful of him, the son of man that you care for him?"

HEBREWS 2:6

Hello Again, Lord ...

Lord, today I surrender my life to your amazing plans.